I ONCE SAW MY HEART

Fred Bazler

Fred Bazler

MINERVA PRESS
LONDON LEICESTER DELHI

ISBN 0 75411 615 8

First Published 2001 by
MINERVA PRESS
St Georges House
6 St Georges Way
Leicester LE1 1SH

I ONCE SAW MY HEART

I would like to thank Eva Bourke, the late Jack Mitchell, Rita Ann Higgins and all the others from the Galway Writer's Workshop who helped me so much in my early attempts at so late an endeavour.

For Beva

Contents

Portraits

Early Days

Irish Sketches

Snapshots

Ageing

Hidden Levels

Others

Quite unintentionally, what I write appears to find its way to a number of distinct categories. In *Portraits* I've written about people of particular interest and importance to me. *Early Days* contains childhood recollections, while *Irish Sketches* reflects my responses to life in Ireland. The poems in *Snapshots* are drawn from my travel experiences; those in *Ageing* are reflections on the effects of time's passing. The poems in *Hidden Levels* draw on subjects of an archaeological/historical nature; and those in *Wonders* relate to the natural world. In *Protests* are poems of a political colouration, and whatever else eludes these categories can be found in *Others*.

I am concerned with the way my experiences can be translated into a written form that animates them into meaning. In doing this, I enjoy travelling that vague border between poetic prose and poetry in search of souvenirs of self-discovery. What I write, I hope, will find a resonance in others.

Fred Bazler
Galway, Ireland
2000

Portraits

Today I Heard Katie Flannagan Died

Today I heard Katie Flannagan died.
I still see each wrinkle in her face
As deep as the nights when reels were lost
In the *scraws* below the slanting rain,
And the sound of feet on hollow flags
Told those deep in the ground
Of life that surged above,
Where the smoking surf from the flaming sea
Blew across the land in shrouds of mist.

She often told of the time when just a girl
She would roll with the boys like the rounded wind
Down the grassy slopes that drop from Doonagore,
And how priest-confronted, she was accused
Of indecencies her greenness was unable to grasp.

When she came to bloom, a hot hungry lad
Led her far beyond lullabies
For children that would never be hers.
While he walked the streets of Broadway.
Only the tired horizon
Wrapped her in its endlessly extending arms.

Alone with her brothers,
Katie watched the passing years, and
Piled the turf
Poked the fire
Picked the eggs

Pitched the hay
Promised her patience
Pined for the past
Plodded to Mass
And prayed to God.

As she fed each evening's fire,
Her wrinkles grew deeper than the fissures
In the rocks of Trá Lán,
Where dark tongues speak of storms and tides;
And pulled across her face like the strings of the sea
That cut into the obliging strand;
Where fresh water streams merge
With the bass that flash beneath the *bodran* beat
That pounds cool white froth
Into the brown-grey grit of the sand.

Now, deep below each season's sigh,
She can hear the rolling boys at Doonagore,
The scratch of rakes saving the hay,
The hoof-thuds of her cows coming home to shelter,
And the bark and paw-patter of her dogs
As they run to greet strangers at the gate.

Oh Katie, if only I could have been close enough to you, to have
at least waved goodbye.

Lilly Vaughan

White-haired and frail Lilly Vaughan,
More a sparrow than a publican,
Would always greet us with alert eyes,
And cock her head to listen intently
To whatever we said,
Pecking in agreement,
Keeping us on our perches,
Waiting until empty glasses
Prompted another round.

Boxes of biscuits and tins of soup,
On the shelves of her tiny shop,
Hardly stopped where her pub began;
But she managed to flit from drinkers to shoppers,
Always with equal ease.

Rosie, the neighbour's child,
Would stand in the doorway waiting for Lilly to say,
'Ah Rosie, me darlin', won't you come in
and give these nice people a song?'
And Rosie, with her head down,
Would walk across the floor
To the shelter of Lilly's wing,
And sing something that sounded
As if it were coming from far inside
Some distant seashell.
Then, with a sweet from Lilly
Bulging out one of her cheeks,
She'd leave without a word.

On the subject of ageing,
Lilly was always fond of saying,
'And why should I be worryin' about that at all...
haven't I always got my *little magic box*?'
And a smile would raise cheeks
Conjured into a pale flush
On either side of her small beak-of-a-nose.

On one visit to Lilly's, we noticed
A large, shiny, coloured photo in a gold frame
Recently placed behind the bar;
And there, in Lilly Vaughan's birdcage-of-a-world,
Looking at us from behind the Mars Bars,
Was the face of someone who'd stepped
Where no one else had ever been.
We leaned closer to read the scrawl
Across his bulging spacesuit.
It said,
To Lilly,
My very best wishes,
    Neil Armstrong

Doolin People

I
Paddy Killourhy
(For Jack Mitchell)

When Paddy Killourhy the fiddler,
Whose nightly jigs and reels
Threaded their path through the smoke and talk
Of McHugh's pub by Liscannor Bay,
Was asked if he had met Richard Burton,
Who had just finished making a film
Not a nod away from where
Paddy and his brother John
Had lived alone for so many years,
Paddy replied,

'No... I don't know him,
but he might know me.
What does he play?'

II
Rory O'Connor

Spuds, bacon and cabbage
From home alone in County Clare
And burgers and French fries
From Boston beaneries
Had made the folds on the back
Of Rory O'Connor's neck
Much like those that hid his belt.

Many schemes, shaped by the moment,
Had made him that *cute*
That once you knew him you could see
How his knowing songs and innocent smile
Could easily be the other way 'round.

One day, he took a donkey in his curragh
Out to Innisheer for the price it would fetch,
A jar or three, and back to the hob
Before it got dark.

In the heat of the haggle,
An Aranman,
Wanting to know the ass's temperament, asked,

'Now Rory, it that donkey quiet?'

'*Quiet... quiet is he?*' Rory answered,
'*sure and isn't he that
quiet he could sleep with the wife.*'

III
Jamesie Woods

Jamesie Woods and his brother Martin
Lived in that little cottage
That balances O'Connor's pub
At the far end of Fisher Street.

Each night when the pub would let out,
We would all cram into Jamesie's house,
Stooping into the gloom
As his turf-fire light
Welcomed the edges of each of our faces.

Whoever had a whistle or fiddle
Would help to make the flags rattle
And the flat grey people rush across
The rough and dusty bumps
Of Jamesie Wood's whitewashed walls.

Never too old to take to the floor
With the tourist girls,
Jamesie would hold his finger
To the side of his nose
As a sign-with-a-wink to tell you
All was well now that visitor's feet
Were stubbing out the sharpness
Of the long winter's silence.

One night,
When the sea had forgotten how to be calm
And the rain pocked its great back
As its white hair flew in all directions,
Jamesie's brother Martin
Was rowing back from Innisheer
To the safety of the shore at Ballyaline.

Jamesie, with a box of matches in his hand,
Walked through the wild night to the quay,
And there, one by one,
Lit his little beacons in the gale.

When his last match had gone out,
And Martin's curragh was nowhere to be seen
In the unravelling rage of the night,
Jamesie, walking home against the wind,
Was overheard to say,

'*Ah… it'll be Ballyaline or the bottom.*'

IV
Packie Russell

Packie Russell,
With larks in his concertina
And troughs and crests
In the tides of his talk,
Could always be found
Near the stone fireplace he'd carved
In Gussie O'Connor's pub,
Receiving visitors who fed him daily
With their crumbs of praise.

He filled us all full
Of genealogies, geologies, geographies,
Histories and hornpipes,
While floating pints or porter
Into the shell of his frame,
Until that twist of a smile
He'd wrapped us all in
Slipped and sank deep
Into the same silence
His music and talk
Had mocked for so long.

Once, one sleepless star-filled night,
We met Packie walking the pale lane
That led him home each evening
From the smoky pub's uproar and jangle,
And listened to him talk
Of constellations and lighthouses,
As his pointing finger
Lost its way in the darkness.

We found him one day
Unable to raise a tune,
As he'd always done
To round the rough edges
Of each grey and lonely day,
A damaged bird in the bushes,
Bruised by the sky,
His fingers resting
On his shiny, soiled trousers.
Just before he left us all,
We heard him say,

'I think I've gone a bit too far this time.'

Mickey Vaughan

I

While others made do
With a hole in a board
In a house behind their own,
Mickey Vaughan made a trough
High on a hill,
Above the farm
That had milked his mother
And father dry
And was his alone,
To catch the rain
And send it through pipes
To a porcelain chamber
Where the pull of a chain
Let water fall
To rush his effluvium
Down a dark whirlpool
That was the wonder
Of all who lived
In the parish
Of Killaspuglonane.

II

While few had a tractor
For the pull and drag
Of each day's drudge,
Mickey had
The parts of two
Scattered all over
His sitting-room floor,
And each step into

Mickey Vaughan's house
Was to walk through an autopsy
Of piston parts,
And carburettor hearts,
And unending entrails
Of springs and coils;
But the search for the source
Of smoke and sputter
Weighed far more
Than any wish to rattle
Across his fields;
And nights were spent
Reassembling parts
Just to learn how
Their fit was proof
Of a certainty
Well beyond the random jolts
Of each weary day's
Toilsome tasks.

III

Not too far
From the spark of turf
In his Stanley No.9 range,
Mickey reserved
The old backseat of a car
Especially for guests,
And sitting there
Among stumps of seed bags
And wrecks of worn-out
Milking machines,
You could see knives and forks
Deep in stratas
Of duck eggs and cabbage
From former meals
Left on plates
That covered the top
Of a table nearby,

And on the wall
A faceless pendulum clock
Loudly ticked on its compassless way
Through each hour of the day,
But if asked the time
Mickey could always tell
By the set of the cogs
The exact time it ever was.

IV

The first few minutes
Of all meetings
With Mickey Vaughan
Had to be spent listening
To him raking his ailments
Into reeks of talk
Of pains starting and spreading,
Rising and falling,
And the chill and fire
Of their itching and swelling.
Then came the denouncing of doctors,
And the disparagement
Of the green and orange pills
He'd gathered in every surgery
Throughout the four round corners
Of County Clare;
And how each prescription bottle
Was tossed away
After one day's trial
Proved their contents to be,

'Totally useless entirely!'

And then more derision of doctors,
Helpless as they were
To disarm the demons
Whose pins and needles
Pierced Mickey's sleep each night
Until he'd wake in an inferno

Under the quilt he'd filled
With the down
From last year's ducks;
And finally you'd have to hear
The cadenza of all his symptoms,
Always ending on the very same note
Of how their cause
Must surely be
The most unknown mystery
In all of County Clare's
Medical history!

V

I once heard Mickey Vaughan
Speaking on the radio
To a nationally-known presenter
Who travelled the *Highways and Byways*
Of rural Ireland
In search of people
He called 'local characters'.
Judging Mickey to be
A fine example
Of one of these,
The presenter held his microphone
Under Mickey's nose,
And with big-city condescension
Carefully wrapped in curiosity and concern,
He enquired:

'Now Mickey, tell me now,
do you believe in the fairies,
you know, *the little people*?'

And Mickey Vaughan,
The man of troughs and flushes,
Pumps, pipes and pistons,
Electrified fences and milking machines
Replied:

'No… I've not come across a-one-of-them,'

But as the conversation
Had taken a turn
To things lacking
In cogs, ratchets or amps,
Mickey added that
He did seem to remember
On one moon-bright night,
Seeing a human skull
Moving slowly across
The road from the cemetery
Just down the way from his farm.
The presenter in his excitement
At this sudden swerve
Off the highways of sheep-talk and silage
And onto the byways
Of the supernatural
Sputtered:

'Yes… yes… and then?'

To which Mickey replied:

*'Sure, but when I picked it up
wasn't there a rat under it,
and all the time pushing it along.'*

VI

The last time I saw Mickey,
He was in his field
On a rare sunny day,
Scything tall grass to stubble.
After his talk of pains and pills,
He asked after the work he'd done
On our cottage
On the sea-side of the land
Not far from his farm.
I neglected to tell him
How last night's rain,

In its probing ways,
Had slipped through the roof he'd built,
And found our foreheads
As we lay awake
In the sleepless dark,
And only replied
That it was, 'grand… just grand…'
And how we couldn't thank him enough
For all the hard work he'd done.
And when the twist of talk
Turned to payment,
Mickey insisted
He'd, 'not take a penny!'
And as I pushed the notes
Into his hand
I could feel how its grain
Told of the hold of hammers,
Shovels, rakes and saws,
For so many years.
Mickey waved goodbye
As I drove down
His long and rutted road
That ended in two concrete pillars,
Each inlaid with sea shells
He'd inlaid there to reflect the headlights
Of night-time visitors' cars.

Each grey post held
Its own half
Of an iron gate
Mickey had made himself
And welded onto the one on the left
Was the letter 'M'
And on the right a 'V',
The rusting monogram
of Mickey Vaughan
The Leonardo of Killaspuglonane.

Grandfather

My grandfather,
With his long black coat,
Black hat, and long white beard,
Stepped from the wrinkled roads
Of his städtel
Into the car-thick, horn-sounding rush
Of a new world
That speeded so heedlessly by him.

As the lid of the Holocaust
Closed Europe into its coffin of terror,
My grandfather, safe among neon-lit
Supermarkets, drugstores and diners,
Brought old tyrannies to a new harbour,
While in his homeland
The arms and legs of neighbours
Entwined in pyramids of frozen postures.

Safe to be himself,
He prayed each day, as he'd always done,
And remained unbending, unalterable,
And set in ways sanctioned by Solomon,
But never realised
That machines, unlike people,
Would not obey him so easily
As his wife and children
Had always done.

Time after time,
The shrill gasp of rubber tyres
And the dull thud of metal on his limbs
Tried to persuade him;
But he wouldn't see
The blood that spattered
His long white beard
And collarless white shirt,
Or the dark red stains,
Almost as lost as his vanished years,
Seeping into the fabric
Of his long black coat.

At the zoo one day,
Looking out from behind my mother's legs,
I watched how the lion, in disdain,
Turned his back on the bar-striped world
Of distant trees and leering faces
That were his landscape,
And allowed his regal tail
To hang carelessly
Outside his cage.

My grandfather,
With mischief tugging at the corners of his mouth,
Reached across the barrier
And with full force,
Pulled the lion's tail
Igniting a roar that almost decomposed
My bird-like bones.
While the lion circled
His insulted dignity,
My grandfather,
With a rare smile of satisfaction,
Chuckled in triumph
As he walked away.

Rubber tyres
Sounded their final warning.
The dull thud of metal issued its ultimatum.
But my grandfather no longer heard them,
Nor saw the blood that spattered
His long white beard
And collarless white shirt,
Or the red stains,
Almost as lost as his vanished years,
Seeping into the fabric
Of his long dark coat.

Grandmother

My grandmother was coaxed
From her Kraków village
To a place where Coca-Cola signs
Blinked red-and-white
Against the night sky.

To my young eyes,
She was always a woman wading in mysteries.

Her hair was not blue-rinsed and curly
Like other grandmothers,
But a dome of her girlhood colour,
Cut and preserved under netting forever,
Over the shaved grey stubble of her head.

Her fingernails were never glazed
Into red-rounded points,
But clipped and kept in a small metal box
To be reclaimed for the afterlife.

Duck feathers from the kosher butcher,
Used for stuffing pillows
And the duvet she and my grandfather slept under,
Carpeted the bedroom floor
Of the wintry room
Where she was suspicious of radiators.

Idle electric light-switches on the walls
Glowed yellow from candles lit at sunset,
While her daily monotone chant
Filled the room,
As she rocked back and forth
Reciting from a little black book
Glancing at it only occasionally.

Her English was just enough
To tell a bus driver
To let her off at the synagogue,
An hour's ride from the Gentile neighbourhood
Her upwardly-mobile children
Had settled in.

Her praying was perpetual,
Always offering thanks
For waking and still being alive,
For food to be eaten,
For food already eaten,
For the safe arrival of midday,
For the health of her husband and children,
For the lighting of candles,
For the time before sleeping,
And between times
She'd travel daily
To a place where she could pray.

Some nights, she'd sit on my bed
And spread out Joseph's coat of many colours
Just for me,
Or tales of wicked Hayman
Who was so cruel to our people,
Or tell me of the heroism of the Maccabees
All in a language I never learned
But somehow always seemed to know.

Some days we'd lunch together
On only potatoes in a bowl.
First I'd watch the yellow butter
Melt into their floury halves,
Then I'd watch water come to her eyes
As she talked about someone called Hitler.

When my grandfather got ill,
She'd heat small glass cups
Over a candle flame,
And like leeches
Stick them all over his back
To 'draw the poison out', she said,
But I never really knew
How it got in there
In the first place.

When he died,
She put pebbles in her shoes
And mornings and evenings
Walked circles for a week or two
All around our backyard.

One winter,
When snow sugared everywhere,
I playfully threw a snowball at her shoulder
She bent down, made one herself
And returned my shot with great accuracy.

Years later, while she was dying,
My mother told her I'd found a girl to marry.
Untrue, of course, but meant to give her
The will to live long enough for my wedding day.

In a hospital room,
On her way to help another patient,
My grandmother coughed red
And then was only the weight
In a box on my shoulder.
My eccentric uncle Max,
Carrying her as well,
Unexpectedly exclaimed,
'Oh, this is a light one!'

I snickered a reflex
And was plunged into guilt
For laughing at such a moment.

I'm so sorry Bubba,
Please forgive me
And let me lay you down now,
Quietly this time.

My Mother Spoke of the Girl She Was

I

My mother spoke of the girl she was
To the boy I can no longer be,
Of following her mother
Down village roads,
A half-day's horse-and-cart ride from Kraków,
To people's houses
To watch her pull babies slowly
Into a world
Where soldiers hawked their killing wares
From town to town,
And bullets burned through her house,
One grazing my mother's auburn hair,
As it was before the way it is
Now so very white.

My mother talked of her raging father,
With his long black beard and stern eyes,
Pulling her by the hair from room to room
In their house,
After a neighbour reported
Seeing the girl my mother was
In the innocence of her years
Talking too freely to a boy
Not of our faith.

My mother spoke of the girl she was
In a city, living with an uncle
Who worked her past the reach
Of her small strength,
And no time to study for school,
Then crossing an ocean

Wider than anything she'd ever seen,
And the smells of steerage, sweatshops
City streets, and tenement rooms
Where one bed was warmth for many;
And how she walked through turmoils
Of Model-Ts and trolleys.

II

My mother, when she was my shelter,
Spoke to the boy listening in me still,
While we made ourselves very small
So not to be found by the stalking beast,
Who was licking Kraków streets
And nearby villages clean
Of all those she knew and loved.
We were hiding far from its evil breath,
Safe in our New England home
With its neatly clipped lawn
And back garden with its silver-birch tree
I was always climbing to see
As far as I could
If the beast was coming near.

III

In Vienna, there's a small museum
That holds remnants
Of an ancient people,
Too reluctant to lose
What little they've left.

A policeman, with an automatic weapon
Strapped to his shoulder,
Paces the cobblestone lane leading to its entrance.
His eyes alert for new outrages,
As if the old ones weren't enough.

Entering, I am watched by a bearded man
With a skullcap,
His eyes filled with apprehension
As he stares at me through bullet-proof glass.
I feel the tightening pull
Of things inside so familiar
But denied and forgotten for so long.

I walk into a dimly-lit room and discover
The neatly-framed faces of Kraków porters
Waiting on ghetto streets to be hired
For carrying loads in their carts.
I see Talmudic scholars
In their long black coats and
Rounded hats trailing twists of hair.
They're conversing on streets
That will soon run red
With the blood of their brethren;
The same streets walked by the girl
My mother once was,
And when asked why she never returned
To visit her native Poland,
The same streets in her mind as she answered,

'I wouldn't know where to step.'

Above the counter near the exit,
The ghetto porters stare at me again
From the shiny surface of a printed poster
Which I buy, put in a mailing tube
And send to my mother with a note saying,

'Dear Momma,
Here's something for you…'

My Father Was a Man of Dreams I Never Knew

My father was a man of dreams I never knew,
Who warmed my small feet in his bed
On icicled Sunday mornings
When frosted windows kept us from seeing
The neighbours outside
Who were so unlike the way we were.

Though he was not often at home,
His presence, like words in a dictionary,
Ensured the safety of my language.

From time to time, I retouch his image
To keep it unlike that sepia smile
He has in the darkness
Of our old photo album.

Seeing the Statue of Liberty,
My father, on his immigration ship,
Waited 'til no one was looking
Then dropped his Communist Party card
Into the waters of New York harbour,
To start a new life, in a new land,
In a new way.

Once, at a picnic with fellow workers,
And aided by too much drink,
He rose to his feet
And began proclaiming tearful words
To all those exiles like him, gathered there.

My mother blushed at his emotive display,
And tried to make him sit down,

But he stood and spoke,
Even though his words were lost
In the noise of everyone there
Too busy foraging for joy
In an alien land
To hear what he had to say.

He talked of things I was too young to know,
Of dreams now lost
So far from where
They first were formed.
Dreams I'll never find.

If only I could have known the shape
Of those tearful words,
Lost in the sound of clinking glasses
Golden with beer in the heat
Of that New England summer.
What could his message have been?

Was it the brotherhood of man?
The solidarity of the proletariat?
The love we should all feel for one another?
The hope for a better life in this new land?

My father was a man of dreams I never knew,
Someone for whom coins were collected
By my schoolmates for flowers.

The flowers arrived,
The neighbours arrived,
The long black limousine arrived,
The autumn arrived,
The snow arrived
And rested on the stone above his head.
Then, warmed by the sun,
It melted into trickles
That soon were no more.

Vraiment, Un Enfant du Paradis

Today Decroux[1] died his second death,
Once movement's captor,
Then, paralysed, its victim,
Now forever its captive.

He walked against the gustless wind,
Defied the dull obstinacy of stillness,
Conjured objects into existence,
And machined his limbs
To climb stairways to nowhere.

Repelling the actor's art,
He danced his own soundless charade,
And with each strain and twist,
Trapezed his way through silence,
Defying weight, mass and void,
Mute-labouring his thrusts and recoils
Until the simplest of tasks
Were unicorned into reality.

He moved so gracefully through the mundane,
Clearing the way for
Barrault and Marceau
To constantly delight us and shape our smiles,

Ah Decroux,
Ce soir, vous êtes vraiment
Un enfant du paradis.

---

[1] Decroux was the great French pioneer of mime, and teacher of Marcel Marceau.

Neighbour

My neighbour, an almost-elderly woman,
Walks on faded carpets among absent people
Whose cold shadows hide her from view.

Only the small sparkle of grandchildren's visits
Brings her briefly into relief
Against the greyness of her long days.

One thing she'll quickly speak of to any new listener
Rises above the plane of her passing talk,
That night, driving home, telling her husband
Bits of news from the day's events,
Suddenly the car left the road
And ended wrinkled against a pole.

He died at the wheel,
Listening, as always,
Without comment,
To her talk.

Just the sound of his name
Lights her face in a moment's flicker,
And then the quiet darkness
Of empty rooms covers her again
Behind the lace curtains
Shielding each window.

My Daughter Talks of Others Finding Love

For Eva

My daughter talks of others finding love,
Of friends so easily fitting puzzle pieces
Into smiling faces of people together.

I find myself remembering
Quests to rescue maidens
Not imprisoned in towers
I bruised myself climbing,
And arriving at parties
Just as everyone else had left.

My daughter talks of others finding love,
And I see only her long blonde plait,
Birthday parties, picnics, puppies in her arms,
A school uniform,
And the face of a young woman
Returning home for the first time.

My daughter talks of others finding love,
And each word is a stone of helplessness
In a wall around me,

But at least I manage to call out a riddle
While I still can be heard:

'What,' I ask, 'when searched for
is never found, and only found when
never searched for?'

'You know,' I say, 'it's like writing a poem.'

Vera

Vera Menchik was by far one of the strongest chess
players in the world during the 1930s, and until she
died in a London air raid at the age of thirty-eight years.

The Irish Times
Chess Puzzle, no. 6215

The game had hardly begun
But Vera's tactical trap was already set.

She left the board
To close the curtains of the shabby room
Only when the sound of the siren
Had become too distracting to ignore,
A trip to the shelter out of the question
Now that knights were angling their way to battle,
And pawns, sacrificed to a greater plan,
Diminished each pattern of pieces
Across the black and white finality of the board.

Vera's face remained unmoved
As her fellow émigré
Advanced his rook into a snare
From which there was no escape.

The light of the lamp nearby,
Unseen by the bombardier above,
Doubled in Vera's soft brown eyes.
She brushed aside strands of her auburn hair
From her forehead,
And conjugated alternatives
In the grammar of her attack.

Just a few more moves and victory was hers!
But wood, plaster, masonry and roof tiles
Rained down on her,
Sending knights, queens and bishops
Into unimaginable positions
Scattered under a blitzkrieg of noise and grey dust.

An old opponent had won with a gambit
That entirely lacked proper development.
Vera, forced to lie beneath a roof beam,
Looked on this rare moment of defeat
With mirrored eyes of disbelief.

Still Life

Decay's punctual scent
Had not yet arrived to Camille,
Who was as still as the table
Beneath the white landscape of her dress,
Her hands two plaited loaves,
Her face a porcelain memory.

Now that mourners had left him
To his long night's vigil,
Claude Monet sat on a bench
Looking at his wife,
Almost believing she was asleep.
Yellow candlelight lost in his beard
Reappeared in the moisture of his eyes,
As he stared intently at Camille's forehead.

Titanium white, he thought,
With just a touch of cerulean blue,
Perhaps a bit of viridian
And even a fleck of ochre...
Warm to cool...
With the slightest highlight
Just off centre...

Suddenly, astonished at himself,
He leaped up and rushed from the room,
Causing the candles to flicker
Their pale cadmium on the walls,
Not too brightly though,
And with just a fleck of ochre.

Artist

He was vain, self-seeking
Superficial and sexist,
Always working
On one canvas after another.

At times his certain blues and greens
Found water and clouds,
And faded far-away hills,
Transforming them into
Deft images of invention.

Other times,
His strokes and shapes
Found only themselves
Making their own form and order
On one canvas after another.

He was a reactionary, an alcoholic,
A womaniser and always scheming for power.
You would never have expected
Such lyricism to scent his work,
But it did,
On one canvas after another.

Then the mouth of a hearse
Opened wide and swallowed him whole.

Death came too soon.
Its opaque colours
Stained the tones of his laughter,
Its pale pigments tinted his lusty ways,
Its matte finish covered him quite uniformly,
Its technique so flawless
Further erasures were hardly necessary.

Retrospective

Staring at the sea,
Watching how waves form their shifting shapes,
A somnambulist awake,
His hands no longer able
To overwhelm pristine surfaces
With smear-slashed, coloured canyons
Or the cruel scumbled smiles
Of his pigment-stroked women.

Primed canvasses are placed in front of him.

Completely unaware he is Willem de Kooning,
He dips his brushes into random colours
And lets them wander,
Trailing across textured whiteness.

He has no idea that tonight
At the Tate Gallery in London
It's the long-awaited opening
Of his major European retrospective.

Self-Portrait

I, of parents who ripped themselves
From all they ever knew,
And stepped still young
From the smells of steerage
Onto the not-so-golden streets of New York,
And made me one hot and sweaty tenement night,
Am a man of no flags.
Like my ancestors,
I've learned the lacy memory
Of each wave's wake.

Spared from the Holocaust,
I've returned to the Old World from the New,
And stand now on your green shore
No longer cargoed and compassed
For unnamed harbours.

I sing odes not anthems,
Admire but do not wear your laurels,
Know the story of your reddened land,
Speak your language in my own way.

Though we are not the same,
The mirror I look into
Holds your face as well.
The shape of your tears no different from mine,
Your laughter sounds much the same.

As for me,
I'm not so much lost
As only displaced
From somewhere I've never been.

Early Days

Seafaring

At an early age
I caught sea fever,
Ran away from home
And worked as a cabin-boy
On the *Pequod*,
Straining with the rest
To sight the sprouting spray
Of that slippery white monster.

Spent a good deal of time
Before the mast,

Loved Madagascar and the Azores,
Crossed the Equator,
Had long talks with the captain of the *Sea Wolf*
Alone in his cabin.

Was cast adrift
From the *Bounty*,

Got friendly with a black man
Aboard the *Narcissus*,

On midnight watch,
Marvelled at how the masts
Of our bobbing ship
Pointed out each constellation,

Saw moonlight
Stipple its long path
Across dark waves,
And how brilliant white caps
Tumbled down breaking peaks,
Shattering into fragments
Of lacy foam,

Pulled halliards,
Pushed the capstan,
Climbed the rigging,
Heard the strain of tackle,
Held onto yardarms
High above lurching decks,
Unfurled flapping sails
Into stiff nor'westers,
Listened to a concertina
Played late at night
In the fo'c'sle,
Stood in the crow's nest
Scanning the horizon
For any sign of land,
Braved catastrophes of surf
'Round Cape Horn,
Lived through downpours
Of a typhoon's rage,
Was becalmed on the Sargasso Sea
Then thrilled to the tug of a breeze
Puffing out our sails
And setting us on our course again,
Sniffed the sharpness of salty gusts,
Sailed past icebergs
Hidden in clouds of frozen mist,
Watched the green after-image
Of the fiery tropical sun
As it dropped below the horizon,

Pitched and rolled
Through legions of breaking waves,
Parted schools of flying fish,
Sighted the first headlands
Under the gull's eye,

Looked for familiar faces
On the dockside
As we moored, loaded with tea and spices,
Nudging the quay's safety at last.

Yes, you might say
I've done some seafaring
In my day.

Recovery

Someone called Jack Frost,
So I was told,
Had painted pale ferns
All over the outside
Of my bedroom window.

In this cold New England winter,
He must really miss the way ferns look
Standing as they do in the shadows,
(Apart from those ordinary weeds
I loved to pull from their sheaths
and put in my mouth, pretending to be a farmer)
To be painting them all over windows like that.

Once everyone's asleep,
I raise the crystal foliage
On this very special night.

The moon eyes me suspiciously,
Wondering why someone my age is still awake
At this late hour,

But I am very busy studying each space
In-between all the stars
For any sign of his sleigh,
His red suit and white beard,
I listen for that laugh
(The one that goes 'Ho, ho, ho'),
And looking for the reindeer
That will land him safely
On my roof, ringed with moon-lit icicles
And mounded with snow.

Cold air yawns through my window
And settles its frosty breath on me
As I wriggle out from under
The duvet my grandmother made,
And try to get a closer look at the sky.
But all my expectations
Are hardly strong enough
To keep sleep from me.

The next morning,
I wake with my forehead flaming.
From outside my bedroom door,
I hear my mother talking to our doctor
About someplace called New Monia...
Nowhere near our neighbourhood
As far as I know...

I have no idea how long
Someone called The Angel of Death,
So I was told,
Waited by my bedside
And wanted to take me somewhere,
But then changed his mind.

All I remember
Is that it was months before
I was well again,

But I've never really recovered
From that empty sky.

Matching

For Gene Reiner

There I am
Only eight years old,
Face flushed,
Wiping sweat
Off my forehead.
I've just cut my lawn.
In my fist a shiny silver coin,
I'm puffed with pride.
My very first paid job!

Along comes my cousin,
A man-of-the-world at sixteen,
Who knows about everything.
I can't resist showing off
My shiny, hard-earned coin,
Hoping to impress him.

'I'll match you for it,'

Says my cousin,
Now holding a coin much like my own
In his hand.
'What do you mean?' I ask.

'It's a game,' he says.
*'We throw both coins up in the air
and when they land, if it's a head and a tail
then they're both yours,
but matching, they're mine.'*

What a fascinating idea, I think.

Up they go
Both coins in the air,
Down they fall
Two silver heads side-by-side
On my newly-cut grass.

It was then,
As he walked away,
With my coin in his hand,
That I first learned
The meaning of matching
Risk with folly.

Two Things My Father Could Do

1

The ordinary household fly was, to me, the ultimate master of escape. All during my fly-hunting days, my self-confidence was constantly undermined by the way this mere buzzing nonentity could so easily elude my very best attempts to capture and totally annihilate it.

My father's accomplishments (despite the excessive hours the poor man had to work to put food on our table) had been undistinguished to me until the day I witnessed a feat, the wonder of which is with me still.

On seeing a fly alight on a chair nearby, my father rose slowly and tiptoed toward it. He cupped his hand just behind the unsuspecting creature (who was busily engrossed in rubbing certain of its legs together); and then there was a sudden *whoosh* of dazzling speed, after which my father's fist enclosed a plaintive buzzing sound. His face was all aglow with a smile of triumph at having captured my complete admiration.

2

At a time when music was almost unknown to me, my father (who would arrive home from work just at my bedtime) would always come to kiss me goodnight. But before he left my room, he would pause in the doorway, lick the fingertips of his right hand and push them along the surface of my door. Their friction would make the most marvellous sound, not unlike the snare drums I'd heard and loved in local parade bands.

These recitals, although always a delight to me, I remember most as the sad percussive fanfares for all my father's evening farewells.

Noah Webster's Finger

I

One day I discovered the dictionary. It wasn't so very long after I'd just learned to read; but no one had ever told me that just one book could corral all the words that ever were, and hold them safely between two large, hard covers.

Many of the words I discovered gave me the same strange feeling I got when seeing the boys who lived just outside my neighbourhood... although I recognised some of them from school, I hardly believed they could ever be my friends.

Passing our Town Hall one day, I noticed a large white statue that had just been put outside this important building.

The big marble lump was, in fact, made to look like the dictionary man, Noah Webster, the one who somehow knew the meaning of every one of those words in the book he wrote. He was completely covered in a marble robe, except for the way his head looked out and one hand hooked its fingers around the large stone book he held; while the other finger, just below his waist, was pointing at something that wasn't there... the way grown-ups often do when they are angry, or telling you not to do something, or trying to say something very important.

II

When I was thirteen, I was given a gift of my very own dictionary. It had my name stamped brazenly in gold letters on its cover, just under Noah Webster's. The first thing I did when I was alone with it was to look up words like 'intercourse' and 'orgasm' and any others of a sexual or scatological nature that I could think of.

One day, a friend of mine took me to a spot just across the street from the Town Hall and positioned me so I could see Noah Webster's statue at a certain angle. It was only then that his pointing marble finger suddenly became a penis that had somehow managed to slip out of his voluminous robes! Much to my gleeful delight, there it was right in front of all the old ladies and young girls who passed it every day and were completely unaware of such monumental exhibitionism!

III

Noah Webster was a linguistic patriot who quickly discovered that the wolf's word for sheep was hardly the same as the sheep's word for wolf. His dictionary was filled with all the flaws and prejudices of any systematic mythology... to say nothing of his excessively alliterative style that would be quite too much even for the most melodic of poets.

Long after I'd broken the ring outside my neighbourhood, and found definitions well beyond the citations and collocations of my early imaginings, I returned on a visit home. Passing the Town Hall, I noticed that someone had broken off Noah Webster's pointing finger.

Irish Sketches

Harbour Visitors

I

Moored in Galway harbour,
A visiting French Navy ship
Has four embossed metal plaques
On the fore and aft sides
Of its main cabin.

In simple white letters
On a dark-blue background,
Honneur and *Patrie*
Face the bow while
Valeur and *Discipline*
Look to the stern.

Obviously,
The French never underestimate
The power of language.

II

An Irish Navy ship named *Aoife*
Floats alongside the quay
That holds back the harbour.

Distant winter waves
In Galway Bay
Are too tumultuous to be breached,
And the ship is now safe from the sea.

On the deck above its bow,
Its only gun
Is a finger warning poachers
And intruding foreign fishing boats alike
Of laws and quotas and territorial waters.

Above its box-like cabin,
A small radar-scanner nods sideways,
Dutifully vigilant
And occasionally receiving impulses
From passing, though not hostile, gulls.

At the top of the gangplank
A smartly-uniformed sailor stands guard.
Only his eyes shift position.

In the stern,
Near bulky forms
White from last night's rare snowfall,
With coal black eyes
And a carrot nose,
Is a snowman.

The Unaligned Man

Driving in Galway one day,
I was alarmed to see an unaligned man
Walking down the middle of St Augustine street
And coming directly toward me!

He was just passing the church,
So comfortably cushioned there by the curb,
And his head, arms and shoulders
Were turned away from his body
While he crossed himself,
As the devout do
When passing a consecrated place.

I quickly put on my brakes
To avoid sending him too soon
To wherever he believed he'd be going
On leaving this world we all know.

He came to a sudden stop just by my bumper,
The screech of my tyres
The sound of his salvation.

His head returned to its customary place,
He produced an apologetic smile
For having his religious fervour
Almost be the death of him.

In Murray's Off-Licence

An old Connemara man
In Murray's off-licence,
Just handed his half-bottle of whisky
By the red-haired counter girl,
Reaches out to her with his,
'*An bhufil tú go maith?*'

She dredges up her,
'*An-mhaith, go raibh maith agat,*'
From the murky depths of her school Irish,
Glancing over at me in assumed complicity.
Aware I am behind him,
The old man turns to me and comments
On this rare sunny day, for this time of the year.
I smile and agree.

The shop owner too busy calculating
Mute columns of ciphers in his ledger,
Is unaware of the loose threads
Entwining the three of us.

The old man turns back to the counter girl
And persists with his, '*Càrbh as tú?*'

'Galway, pure Galway,'
Is the girl's pert reply,
This time in English.
Looking over his shoulder,
She asks me,
With her quick spark-of-a-smile,

'What'll it be?'

'I'll have this bottle of red wine,' I answer,
Wondering why my own language
Suddenly sounds so strangely foreign.

Ready to leave,
But not moving from his spot,
The old man says, '*Slán agat anois.*'
'*Slán,*' she answers,
Her glance still trying to enclose me
In the boundaries of her unease.

The Connemara man walks slowly out of the shop
And steps onto the cold rebuff
Of the hard grey pavement,
Outside Murray's off-licence,
Below the speechless clouds
Slowly passing over us.

Days in the Burren

There are days in the Burren
When three kinds of clouds
Change places
Across a grey sky that's blue,

When hesitant rain
Pulls the sky's frayed edges
Towards limestone hills,

When the sudden sun's flash
Surprises shadows into sight,

Where memories of rainbows
Haunt the smoking sky.

There are days in the Burren,
Days like this.

In Connemara

Uninvited grey roads
Dismay the grass
And perplex the sheep.

Carefully stringed brown poles
Contradict the enumerate sweep
Of the landscape.

Sudden winter cars
Rearrange the silence
That rests heavy
In Connemara.

The Meeting

In the railway station,
A short blond man
Holding a handle attached to a honey-coloured dog,
Nudges his way through brushes and bumps,
Alongside the screeching stop of a train.

At the far end of the platform,
A tall man wearing dark glasses,
Steps from the coach
And into a stream of shoulders and elbows
Pulling him along and knocking him off-course
As he parts his way, with his long white cane,
Through the noisy crowd
And toward the blond man and his dog.

They both thread a path
Through confusions of people until
They meet, perfectly.

Greeting each other with unseen smiles,
The blond man takes his friend's arm,
And the honey-coloured dog
Leads them both home.

The Returned Red-Haired Girl

A red-haired girl
Labours her way through
The airport's arrivals door.
Her eyes, beacons of anticipation,
First find her little brother.

She drops her suitcase,
Then orbits him up in her arms,
Revolving him around and around,
Landing him gently back on the ground.

Her hungry arms devour
First her sister,
Then her mother,
Then her father,
Pressing out the cruel time
And the harsh space
Too long between them all.

Her face aflame,
Her eyes shining
On each of her own,

The returned red-haired girl
Home in Ireland,
Just for a visit.

Signs

For Fergus Bourke

Long before Connemara,
A narrow road twists
Off the straighter and smoother one to Oughterard,
And loses its composure over wavy bog land,
Where pale-blue trenches branch from the roadside
And its neatly-piled ziggurats of turf.

A small green *An Post* sign nailed to a pole
Points to an ordinary-looking house
That's grown a wardrobe-sized room
Where we stand talking to the post-mistress,
Who has just left her washing
To sell us a jar of coffee
From her little post-office shop.

'On holiday?' she asks.

'Sort of,' I reply.

'Bad weather,' she continues.

'We must be brave,' I quip.

'It's not brave but waterproof
we need to be,'
She replies with barely a smile.

Three cars parked outside
What seems to be someone's home.
Only the word 'push' on the door
And piles of silver-coloured beer-kegs at the back
Hint at what this place might be.

We push the door
And find clusters of farmers
Talking around a turf fire,
A rugby scrum on the telly,
And a woman padding back and forth
In her house slippers, behind the bar,
As she draws pints of Guinness
For her customers.

We order drinks and sit down at a table,
Inconveniencing the black sheepdog under it
Who reluctantly makes room for our feet.

The road outside, calm by now,
Finds a small quay by the lake nearby,
Where pastel-coloured rowboats
Lie overturned and lifeless
In the November chill.

Windows of empty caravans
Stare out at a heron
Hiding between rushes.
Two distant swans are white specks
On the far shore of the lake.

An angular building,
With a cross on top of its brutally-clipped forms,
Hacks its slants and angles
Around stained-glass windows.

From its roof, three tubular speakers
Impersonate church bells in a belfry.
Below, a heavy front door, closed as a coffin,
Opens only on Sundays.

A hawk flutters high above us.
A cat on a stone wall
Pays very close attention
To each move we make.
Chickens congregate outside bungalows
Designed by number from a catalogue.
A bull glances up at us briefly
Then continues nibbling grass.

To me this is a place filled only
With innuendoes of silence
And implications of remoteness,
But ask almost anyone
Anywhere near Galway,
About this place
And they're bound to say,

'Sure and doesn't everyone know Collinamuck!'

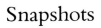

Snapshots

In the Naturhistorisches Museum, Vienna

For Sigfrid and Gerda Fäerber

A boy with black curly hair and large brown eyes
Randomly orbits the glass dome
Set neatly into the museum floor
As a cloudless sky for the bone people
Who lie below, suspended in soil,
Exactly as they were found;
The mother's stick arms still holding her child
For this longest of journeys.

Late-morning light through tall baroque windows
Searches the dim hollow
And finds the bone-child's small white teeth,
So perfectly formed yet hardly used,
Causing their brightness
Against his dull grey skull,
Sparsely decorated by a thin dark line
That zigzags its way across it.

The brown-eyed boy above,
Quite unaware of the scene below him,
Runs off to find his mother.

Broken Symmetry

October Sunday afternoon,
Muscovites leave their towers
To visit the ruins
Of a lavishly brutal past.

Intruding through Prince Kuskovo's gate,
Past birch-tree sentries,
They walk the grounds circling a lake,
That holds the drift
Of the cloud's easy conjuring,
And stroll through the forest
That once was home to 200,000 serfs.

Only the rasp of the gravel path
Announces the arrival of all those
Curious to see the wooden palace,
And walk its dim corridors,
Watched over by darkened faces
In tarnished golden frames.

In the palace gardens,
A man and his twin daughters
Walk where balanced topiaries
Once shielded flirtations and intrigues.

Heedless of history and the grand symmetry
Of paths and pavilions around them,
One child holds her father's hand tightly
While the other strays adventurously ahead,

The price of their admission already paid for
Long before they arrived.

Kiev Ozymandias, 1991

Two vast and trunkless legs of stone
Stand surrounded by scaffolding,
While workmen in red metal hats
Subtract from the torso of a colossus
That once walked the world.

Two giant feet, so long astride the city,
Point to a long stairway down a hill,
Past the Lenin House of Culture,
Across Lenin Avenue,
And on to Lenin Square
Where, ringed by plumes of fountains
And surrounded by blue and yellow flags,
Small circles of people gesture and argue,
Intoxicated with their newly-discovered voices.
Elsewhere, they congregate
Chanting amid incense and candles.

The statue's immense missing head and body
Are nowhere to be seen,
Not even nearby
On the lone and level sands
That stretch so far away.

Anniversary Procession in Dnepropetrovsk

Marchers with skullcaps and prayer shawls
Carry candles that light faces on photos
Of friends and relatives
Absent but unforgotten.
The procession's little lights flicker
As all walk slowly in remembrance
Of boxcars and the camps,
Bombings and betrayals.

This grass!
These trees!
Fill your eyes with them!
You are now their eyes.
Speak out!
You are now their voices.

And remember well
How easily candles
Can be snuffed out
By a bitter wind.

The Dnieper

A river like any other,
A bit wider perhaps.
Old men fishing from its sides,
Casting their time away,
Throwing back what they've caught.

A bridge like any other,
Bending from bank to bank,
But topped with a large red star.

Apartments like any other,
With windows overlooking the river.

A sky like any other,
But with clouds too soiled
To allow the sun to come through.

A river like any other,
Ripples wrinkling its surface
As it flows down from Chernobyl.

At the End of Sharia Al-Ahran

I

The traffic-infested road of Sharia Al-Ahran
Starts straight and wide
From the western bank of the Nile.

Its cracked and pitted pavement
Covers funeral processions
Of priests who once raised dust
That settled on pharaohs' coffins.

Now, processions of tourist buses drive along it
And disgorge passengers into souvenir shops
To buy authentically-faked images
Painted on real papyrus.

Grocery shops along the busy road
Are filled with baskets of red petals
And ochre-coloured powders.

Women sheathed in black
Carry bundles on their heads
To decaying apartment buildings
Whose balconies are festooned
With limp and drying underwear.

Tribes of boys play football on wasteland
Filled with pyramids of rubbish
And abandoned cars.

Men sit in small cafés all day
Drinking red-tinted *kirkaday*,
And talking idly
As they swish and click their worry beads.

Each evening,
Tourists cram into nightclubs
That line the street
To gape at rolls of flesh
Quivering to over-amplified music.

II

Above the last soiled buildings
At the end of Sharia Al-Ahran,
First, two peaks loom pale
Against an unblemished sky.
Then three pointed stone mountains
Dwindle you into insignificance
As you look up from their shadows.

Once, so smooth,
Each of their slanting blocks of stone
Could flash a spark
Too fierce for any eye to catch,
A dazzle that could command
The furthest shore of the vast sandy sea
Where they're anchored;
Now pitted and worn, still a wonder.

In their core,
Space enough for just one man,
Who lived beyond toil,
A god on earth,
Whose gaze could never be met;
Someone who sent soldiers to enslave distant empires;

And after the ebb of his years
Found a home in a stone box
Ringed with incantations,
Certain his *ka* would voyage to the bosom of Osiris
And live forever in the sparkle of his constellations.

III

The wonder of these pedestals for eternity
Is more in their hubris than their size.
While each peak was valued for immortality,
Their cost is beyond calculation.

Though their bones are robbed and lost,
Each pharaoh's delusions are kept alive
In the gasps of even the most world-weary tourists,

And schoolchildren throughout the world
Still learn the names of Chephren, Cheops and
Mycerenius.

Luxor Scene

Breeze drifter
Smoothes the sky,
A hawk glides.

Feather flourisher,
Hovering blur of wings,
A hummingbird above rushes.

Floating white triangles,
Silent on the blue drift,
Feluccas sailing.

Old moist mother,
Wide and welcoming,
The Nile passes
Below the Valley of the Dead.

Dying king in the sky,
Fire-disc rolling slowly,
The sun is lost.

No other sunset
Will ever be
Innocent of all this.

Riccordo di Roma

The walls of Rome
Stand like haggard legionnaires
Peering into Dacian mists
For signs of marauding Celts,
Whose torques glint golden
In the cold northern light
Piercing low grey clouds.

The walls of Rome
Shudder slightly as jets to far destinations
Leave vapour trails across blue and cloudless skies.

The walls of Rome still stand long after
That man of celestial yearnings,
Who never saw this impressive stone display
Or the stern faces of men
Who tortured the innocent,
All in His name.

The walls of Rome cast long shadows
Where black-shirted men of angular stride
Once thirsted for a glory gone,
And marched as ruthless
As the worst of their ancestors,
Until a cord tugging their ankles
Made their bulging eyes see the world upside-down,
And blood clot on their faces
As it flowed from mouth to hair.

The walls of Rome stand patiently
As twittering tourists' cameras
Chirp like the beaks of birds
That over-punctuate each evening sky
Above the Piazza della Repubblica.

The walls of Rome shrunk to minute innocence
On the map I've brought back to where
Marauding Celts came to rest,
Their torques glinting golden
In the cold northern light
Piercing low grey clouds.

The Church of Sant'Antimo

For Roberta Angeletti

New Year's morning
In the church of Sant'Antimo
Surrounded by Tuscan hills
Silvered with frosted olive groves
That pause at roughly-ploughed soil.

Charlemagne's troops took ill here.
The Emperor vowed that if the sickness passed,
He'd build a church on this spot,
And here is Sant'Antimo.

I sit inside listening to the winter wind
Blow past its half-opened door.
At the altar,
Five monks cocooned in white robes,
Wrap themselves in smoking incense
And entwine their severe chant
Around the few of us
And the splayed man hanging
Above their intimacy.

The roof with its wooden ribs
Sails on its ancient course,
We the cargo, far from the shore,
Fixed in place like a serpent's victim
Or one held in a lover's stare.

I sit and sail beyond the cross
To somewhere searched but seldom found,
Somewhere I have never travelled before.

The First Ghetto, Venice

Two arcs of iron foliage
Painted green
Bridge a pale-blue canal.

I walk the wooden slats they enclose,
Stepping on forgotten sounds
Of shoes returning from the Rialto by curfew time,
On percussive high-heels,
Dull shufflings and light patterings,
Followed by the thud of jackboots
And muffled sobs fading away.

I am only a visitor,
Someone apart, but still a part
Of what I see.

A tranquil square warmed by the Venetian sun.
The sound of *kletzmer* music from a corner shop.
Commemorative panels sculpted in relief
On the surrounding walls,
Lines of people filing into boxcars.
A firing squad, executions.

An upstairs synagogue,
Not allowed the show and glitter
Of Santa Maria della Salute
Or the Byzantine splendour of San Marco,
Only a simple worshipping place
With its woman's gallery
For looking down on the men at prayer.

On its floor,
A pattern of inlaid marble
Is regular until it reaches the exit,
Then its design goes askew.

'Why has the pattern changed so abruptly?'
I ask our guide.

She replies,

'They believed only God could be perfect.'

Sicily

For Riccardo Vagliasindi

I

Catania streets cover
The traces of Hellenes,
Saracens, Normans and Bourbons alike,
Then Garibaldi's Thousand,
With their red shirts
Like Etna's flame,
Returned the island
To its Roman line,
Then left it drifting
From the mainland,
A precarious place
Caught between a volcano
And a Black Hand,
A land of cactus thorns,
Lemon trees, and broken columns
Of Doric temples.

II

Etna's white wings
Rest on the highest hills
Above olive groves;
A plume of cloud
Trails from its beak
Sharp winds cool its slopes.
Its heart holds a thunder
That can spew strings of fire
High into the night sky,
And make smoking orange rivers

Flow down its sides,
Turning trees into grotesque
Black creatures frozen in stone.

III

In Siracusa
Ancient laughter still lingers
In trees that shadow
The stepped marble slabs
Where farmers and tradesmen,
Artisans and statesmen delighted
As young Aristophanes' characters
First came to life.

In the city square,
A naval officer's wedding day,
In his dark-blue uniform,
With its shiny black belt,
Sword and scabbard,
And wide white sash
Across silver buttons,
He bends his arm stiff
For his bride to hold.
They walk past an overstuffed baroque church,
Her face flushed in triumph and pride,
The long train of her wedding gown
Trailing along the rough grey cobblestones
Like the mist that moves through
The island's empty inland valleys.

IV

Nato's streets
Have lost their stains
Where the *nobili*
And the voiceless clashed.
Earthquakes have tumbled
Churches and palaces,

Each time rebuilt
With greater grandeur,
As if to show nature
Who really rules
In this part of the world.

On a hill above the city square,
Leering stone satyrs
And imaginary animals
Support the balconies
Of an appropriated palace,
Now used as a library.
In one of its many rooms,
A talkative librarian
Makes more noise
Than all the chattering schoolgirls
Studying at plain wooden tables
In the extravagantly-spacious room.
On the ceiling above their talk of boyfriends
And school assignments,
Apollo chases Daphne
In their frozen tableau
Of unconsummated action.

Led down a narrow street
And to a large house,
I am introduced to an aged but active
Retired doctor from Rome.
The pains of the over-privileged
Have enabled him to buy this palace
Of the lesser *nobili*.
Where we walk together
Over patterned tiles
Through rooms of vanished opulence and *ennui*,
And come to a rococo bedchamber.
On either side of the over-stuffed bed
Are two doors to changing rooms
Where husband and wife undressed

Before entering for lovemaking or sleep;
Nakedness being only for images of Persephone
Carried off by Hades
From the painted ceiling above
To the underworld below.

Because we speak English,
The doctor's wife serves us tea,
Instead of the rich dark coffee
We love so in Italy.
From deep in his armchair,
The doctor issues orders
To his neatly-groomed wife,
Who has shared his long, and at times,
Eventful life for so many years.
She interrupts his talk, of the weather
And who is in old framed photos
Carefully placed on furniture around the room,
With urgings of almond biscuits
Just delivered this morning
From the corner *pasticceria*.

The doctor walks us to the door.
The tap of his cane punctuating
His cheerful pleasantries.

Later we learn of his forgetfulness;
He had neglected to show us
His most treasured possession,
A photo with Mussolini's arm around his shoulder.

V

In the fishing village of Cefalj
Tentative morning light
Tints the rough edges of a mountain
Above the coast road to Palermo.
In a glance away,
Blue-violet shadows

Have turned to olive green;
Clusters of small houses
At the foot of the mountain
Have changed from pale grey
To the white of waves
Arriving on the shore.

VI

At night,
Palermo's dark stone churches
And hulking buildings
Watch us from behind streetlight shadows
That hide their fearful secrets.

If cities had a gender,
Palermo would be male and hard,
Brutally strong and unwilling to yield.

Inside the dome above the altar
In the church of Monreale,
Gold and coloured mosaics merge
To form the face of Christ the Pantocrator.
His one hand holds the Scriptures.
The other, with two fingers raised,
Blesses the believers
And faithless alike,
As they gape up at His sheer size
Black beard, and dark penetrating eyes.

VII

Enna, in the heart of the island,
Keeps company with the clouds.
I am a bird looking down to scan the way
The little hill towns diminish and fade
Far off in all directions to the horizon.

Posing as a triangular cloud,
Etna, on the other side of the island,
Floats silently in the distant sky
Alone above the rounded landscape.

VIII

Elephants, hippos and giraffes
Are being loaded onto barges.
Girls in bikinis are at the seaside,
Cupids are flying above lovers' intimate talk.
Lions and leopards are attacking helpless gladiators,
Stags and wild boars flee from their hunters,
And geometric illusions reverse themselves
All in mosaics on the floors
Of the house in Piazza Amerina
Where the regional governor once lived,
A man who was almost Emperor.

IX

In Agrigento,
Greek temples are illuminated
Against the night sky.
Laurel trees line the old Roman road
That lingers through the town;
Hedges of rosemary
Are interrupted by cacti
Protecting their prickly pears;
Olive trees rustle their silver leaves
In a gentle breeze
As I leave Sicily.

La Primavera, Florence

La primavera quando flora di fiori adorna il mondo

Lorenzo di Medici

The pale-blue man with puffed cheeks
Is winter's lust.
His hands, searching for warmth,
Reach out to grasp
The young woman of ripening flesh,
Fecund as the patient earth.
His touch blossoms into her breath of flowers.
They fall from her mouth onto the sleeping soil
With the certainty of each new season's impulse,
And land on the robe that leads
To the face of Spring
And her smile like the triumph of roses.

Nearby,
Venus, crowned with foliage,
Surveys her subjects.
Above her, blindfolded Cupid flies,
Carefully aiming his flaming arrow
At the most wistful of the three dancing sisters,
Who will soon grow passionate in their beauty
And beautiful in their passion.

Unconcerned,
Mercury, detached from the others,
Knows what's beyond the torpid clouds
He parts with his staff,
To see what makes the pale-blue man
With puffed cheeks,
Search for warmth.

Reaching for the young woman
Of ripening flesh,
Fecund as the patient earth.

On Seeing the Parthenon

Pride of Pericles,
Sheath of Athena's icon,
Your fluted fingers
Worn, white, spot lit
Against the night sky,
There above the Pláka and passing traffic.

You were possessed by Romans
Profaned by Christians,
Defaced by Turks,
Your sides blasted away by cannon fire,
Then your English admirer
Came to pick your crown clean.

There you are on your rocky plinth
That holds the stilled voices
That once spoke so well
Of an abducted wife and all that followed,
Of a wanderer finally returning home,
Of the thunderer of Olympus,
And a blinded king.

Theorem in stone,
Parable of perfection,
Syllogism in marble,

You were the very mould,
Pivot and cradle
For all that followed.

Take Me Out to the Ball Game
(Camden Yard, Baltimore, Maryland)
For Leah Kelly

I, a visiting Van Winkle,
Look at the half-closed lids of dim lights
Boxed high in the black Baltimore night,
Above us in Camden Yard,
As we wait for the lurch of the large clock
And the ball game to begin.

In the hot darkness,
A low-flying plane trails pinpoints of light;
Jake's Seafood Restaurant, $15.00 specials...
Here, not even the skies are safe from capitalism.

Below us, the grass is the greenest of greens,
Carefully-cut and cared-for
From the wide outfield
To the infield's precise geometry
Of raked soil studded with three
Small white bases.
We wait for the ball game to begin.

The grey repetition of stadium seats
Gradually becomes a speckled array
Of blues, greens, yellows, whites and reds,
As each row is filled,
And we all wait for the ball game to begin.

Suddenly, hundreds of suns cheat the night,
And daylight is ours!
The players are on the field,
And the crowd is one voice of shouts and chants,
Merging with calls
Of beer and hot-dog sellers
Walking up and down the aisles,
As the ball game begins!

The pitcher on the mound,
Arms stretched high above his head,
Goes into his wind-up,
Kicks a leg out into the hot night air,
And throws his fast balls, drops and curves.
The small white dot-of-a-ball
Shoots its leathery echo to us
From the catcher's mitt,
Or flies with a crack from the batter's bat
That ignites the crowd
And sends a runner to third.

Sizzling ground balls, lazy pop-ups,
Fouls, Texas Leaguers, line drives
Grand-slam homers, and double plays,
Three and two, walks, strike-outs,
Top of the seventh, bottom of the eighth,
Innings pass in grid-like regularity
As each side is retired
And the other comes to bat.

And all 45,000 of us,
Unconcerned by nine-to-five,
Or why we are,
Or tarnished childhoods,
Or impeded hopes,

Or expatriate pangs,
All sing in unison
Along with the full voice
Booming from speakers
Somewhere above our heads;

'For it's one, two, three strikes and you're out at the ol' ball game.'

Glenwood Springs, Colorado

For Ruth and Joe Kaplan

Aspens melt green to yellow
Above an emerald palm
That holds the vacant sky.

Legions of spruce,
Unvanquished by the sharpness of a sudden autumn.
Guard the wilderness where we are intruders
Walking paths where bears have clawed wild berries
Into their mouths,
And beavers made hourglass cuts in tree-trunks
To pull and pile them on heaped tangles
Stopping the rush of a persistent stream.

In the sky above the timber line,
A hawk glides in parabolas
And looks down on the battlements of maroon mountains.
His eyes hold peaks that shade the chill
Of patient snowdrifts.

He scans the valleys
Where wild flowers were once stained
By the killing and the killed,
And blood clotted the crust of a garden
For those who first found this land
And held it close to them
Before it was taken away
By rabbles of blue-coated soldiers
And settlers fresh from Independence Pass,
Who came to scratch their Leadville,
Coleville, Marbleville and Goldville

Out of the abundance of mountains,
Mesas, canyons and plains,
And soak themselves
In the hot sulphur springs at Glenwood.

Prospectors drifted into the quiet valleys
Heated and frozen by the blaze and snows
Of each passing season,
Thirsting always for the sun's light made solid,
Blasting mountain-sides into astonished mouths,
Spewing avalanches of shattered rocks,
Frightening the fragile deer,
Clawing shale with their raw fingers,
Washing what they'd found
In white-water rivers
Swelled by rain and melting snow,
Dropping down gullies, past sullen rocks.

Tumbled cabins,
With their bleached beams pecked by axe-marks,
And sad jumbles of decaying logs
Are all that's left of the young adventurer's homes.
They came to make a quick fortune
But many returned penniless.

Now, the hawk's eye holds
Long straight highways pointing to ski resorts,
Chalets and condominiums, diners and gas refineries,
Tall buildings and airport towers,
All seeming strangely temporary,
Still in a wilderness of such profusion,
There should have been land enough for everyone.

Manhattan Snapshots

For Mike Frank

I

I walk between mountains
That mimic pieces of sky
At passing clouds,

Buzz of international commerce

Parting manufactured mist
Rising from iron grates
Set in flattened Manhattan meadows,

Shouts and foreigners in conversations on the streets

Alongside buses, cars, and taxis
Moving towards some secret pollen,

Bumble of Yellow Cabs

I thread through
Shades and shapes of people
Walking, looking, eating, talking,

Urgent whine of police-car sirens

Past windows where motionless men and women
Pose in the latest cut
Of Armani, Calvin Klein and Gucci,

Shrill pleading of an ambulance separating traffic

Past windows where laptop computers, calculators,
Personal organisers, watches and sound systems
Are all available at 'The Lowest Prices in Town!'

Shrouded silence of stretch limos passing

Along the floating hive
Held by fingers of bridges,
The only imperative;
To buy to sell,
To sell to eat,
To eat to live,
To live to sell,

Here the dollar is honey

II

I see tundras of concrete
Rise in reversed icicles
Dripping their ingenious forms
Into the sky
The Chrysler Building, the Empire State,
The World Trade Center with its twin towers,
The tallest of all.

Central Park,
An oasis of foliage
Where the wealthy pay to look down
To see their children walked and wheeled
By maids with foreign accents,
Dodging the rush of skaters and joggers.

As soon as it rains,
Peddlers appear on the sidewalks
Selling umbrellas outside shops
Where they must pay to stand.

Downtown,
Almond-eyed women are machines
That cut and stitch all day
Until sleep comes in beds
Still warm from someone else.

Uptown,
Are shops opened only
For those allowed to buy by appointment.

Eighty thousand or more
Mostly women and children,
Live in patched-together houses
On the streets,
Trying to keep warm and dry.

Gamblers, with pockets filled with cash,
Waiting on a bus to leave for Atlantic City
Are all robbed at gunpoint
By a thief of great initiative.

The unfinished bulk of a cathedral
Is dragged into a new millennium
Looking backward to Gothic wonders
From the Old World.

Teenagers play basketball in rare spaces
Shadowed by apartment blocks
With waiting list of years
Before you can live
On the thirty-seventh floor.

A gay and lesbian synagogue
Is near Malcolm X's former mosque.
Tibetan monks worship in their
Staten Island monastery
Looked down on by the Statue of Liberty.

A bar proclaims its antiquity
With a sign saying 'Founded 1977'.
Everywhere, everyone is eating
Korean, vegetarian, Tex-Mex, sushi,
Steaks, linguine and clams,
Pizzas, bagels, hamburgers,
Foot-long hot dogs,
Six-inch-high pastrami/chicken liver/
Swiss-cheese sandwiches for one,
Extra bowls of pickles and coleslaw free.

In the Waldorf Astoria bar,
Margaritas, Singapore Slings, dry Martinis,
Bloody Marys, and Grasshoppers.
Outside the entrance,
Crowds have been waiting for hours
To catch a brief glimpse of an arriving pop-star.

The Guggenheim
Coiled by the sidewalk,
Guards its own exclusivity.

The Frick mansion
On Fifth Avenue,
Looks down its nose on the street by the park.

The chandeliers at the Met
Pulled up to the ceiling
Just before the opera is about to begin.

Macy's at springtime
Festooned with real flowers,
Their scent competing with the perfume counters.

Rockerfeller Center skaters,
Legs like compasses,
Scratch their geometry into the ice.

A huge Calder mobile
Moving slowly in the JFK Aer Lingus hall,
Insinuating flight patterns.

The roar of take-off,
Looking down on the hive
And everyone busy making money.

Harbour Island Beach, the Bahamas

Its history of stone,
Forgotten in pink granules,
The sand sounds
An eternal percussion
From pale turquoise waves
Washing in from Africa,
And tugging its strands
Back into a watery retreat.

Its fickle memory
Easily recalls our footsteps,
Or shoe sole geometry,
And tells of trailing,
Forked prints of seabirds
Pecking at dark strips of stubble
All along the pale beach,
Whose scalloped ridges echo the shape
Of last night's gusts of wind.

It clings affectionately
To our hands and feet,
And finds its way
Into the most remote crevasses
Of clothes and skin.

Obligingly, it agrees to be
A turreted castle
Ringed with a watery moat,
Reached by a sandy highway
Tunnelling through an archway entrance,

Or easily becomes
An alligator, or turtle,
Or even a reclining nude
With her small dunes pointing
Up towards a cloudless sky.

It parts to hold a toddler's wading pool,
Or is made into a fortress
Bravely defending the shore
From assaults of foaming waves
That inevitably melt its walls,
Like ice cream, into the sea.

Proudly, it displays souvenirs of rope,
Fisherman's glass floats,
Bits of wood from forgotten ships,
Or shows off washed-up tree trunks
With grey branches smoothed by the sea.

Adaptable, accommodating, curious, responsive,
Inventive, covetous, intrusive,
The warm sand allows us to embrace it
In search of rest and peace.

Ageing

I Once Saw My Heart

I once saw my heart,
A puffing bloated fish
Staring through the glass limits
Of its small galaxy;
And I could see exactly how
My deep red breath,
Expanding that contracted form,
Made all the colours
Of my universe possible.

Often, when a heart rebels,
It's attacking itself,
Forcing its carrier to consider
A life clogged by discord,
And too empty of the fullness of those who feel.

Often, when the heart
Of one defeated and degraded
Shapes itself into its oppressor's mould,
It causes its own destruction,
But oh-so-slowly
With only a down-turned smile
To announce its end.

The Ancient Egyptians,
Knowing the heart to be
The pivot of all our inner constellations,
Believed it must be outweighed
By *ma'at*, the feather of truth
Before its owner could enter the westernmost lands
Beyond the sound of all its beating.

Studying the pulsating glow,
I searched the screen
For the remnant flags of victory,
Or the scarred welts of defeat
That are the counterpoint of who I am,
But the nurse turned off the scanner
And all I could see was only my face
Reflecting back at me.

The Young

The young have blood
That boils in veins
Untroubled by the sweet ravages
Of raising children.

The young have not heard
The voiceless years pass,
As silent as dead friends
Who no longer read
The letters we send them daily.

The young have yearnings
Unlike the old
Who yearn less,
As they grow grey, dusty and frayed,
Like the books they've shelved
So long around them.

The young have tongues
That taste tastes untainted by knowing
They'll never be tasted again.

The young have palms
That have not yet felt
That almost familiar touch,
Lost when grown children leave
From long, cold platforms.

The young hear no echoes of voices
Returning to remind them
Of all their forgotten wishes.

The young have hopes,
Shadowed by the closeness
Of what comes too soon
Not knowing what comes too late.

For a while, time is their slave,
But they are the moment's captive.

Masquerade

Quite clever
How my older sisters,
Not seen for so long,
Have put on grey wigs,
And pencilled lines
That web their faces
With such skill
I hardly recognised them,
But they never mentioned
Anything about a Masquerade.

A friend of mine from my teens,
Visited after so many years,
Has used a pillow or something
To make himself into
An overfed old man;
And the pale highlights in his hair
Quite effective in completing his disguise,
But he never mentioned anything
About a Masquerade.

My children,
Away from home so long,
Have even managed to alter
Their shapes and faces,
Ah, but they always were so good
At dressing up in disguises.
I wonder what they didn't tell me
About the Masquerade?

My wife,
Whose face I study every day,
Has changed her cheeks and chin
So seamlessly, I hardly noticed
How she's decided to go to the Masquerade.

Funny, she's usually very good
About reminding me
When there's a party to go to.

I Rushed Myself to the Casualty Ward

I rushed myself to the casualty ward.
'Yes, can I help you?'
Nurse, something is seriously wrong with me!
'Name please.'
Autumn is tugging at my leaves! I'm losing them from my branches!

'Address?'

Winter has already reached my beard!

'Do you have health insurance, sir?'

Now the frost is covering my hair!

'Would you please take a seat over there.'

You don't understand, this is serious!
I'm beginning to forget how to remember!

'The doctor will see you in just a moment.'

I'm always thinking of what it will be like
to be beyond all thinking! My face is a parody
of my old passport photos! Nothing is
the way it's always been!

'Been waiting long?'

Yes for a while now, you see, the presence
of the past is obscuring my future!

'My lad here has a fractured arm, I think.'

My children no longer look like themselves!

'Mr Fred Bazler, the doctor will see you now.'

Something has happened to my shape!
My chin sags and my waist is swollen!

'Come this way please.'

Where will all my memories go? My youth is a
misplaced fiction!

'Hello, yes, now Mr Bazler,
What seems to be the trouble?'

A Few Incantatory Words

For Beva on our 30th Wedding Anniversary

A few incantatory words
Changed us so
From ourselves
To what we were to be to each other.

That day,
You brought your wide-brimmed hat,
The dowry of your singularity,
To shade us both
From the glare of our loneliness.

The road beneath us
Moved quickly away
From the simple ceremony
In the house of friends.

With the car windows open,
The wind blew your hat away.
Why, we wondered, stop to reclaim something
We had so willingly lost?
And so we hardly looked back
To see where it landed.

With the wind in your hair,
We were too filled with each other
To feel the road beneath us,
And lost our way, arriving much too late
At a seaside inn, with no reservations.

The owner, still covered with sleep,
At first refused a room,
But relented when she heard
That a few incantatory words
Had changed us so from what we were
To what we had only just become.

Why was the touch of you that evening
So much unlike before,
And yet so still the same?
Your flesh, bewitched by
A few incantatory words,
Now wrapped us both
In its gentle sorcery.

In the morning, we walked along the beach
As waves, like inquisitive relatives,
Arrived to inspect the shore,
Where we started, alone but together,
On our way to discover each other.

Sixty-Third Autumn

Gashes of leaves
Crimson welts across
The year's dying flesh,

Gales through
Garden furniture
Overturned in a courtyard
Bereft of summer,

Dishevelled waves
Unsettle the horizon,

Chimneys whistle
Their white breath,

Strings of rain
Plucked by gusts,

Sixty-three lost leaves
As another falls.

Retirement

Down from office shelves,
Books edged with dust
Clinging too fast
To be easily blown away;
Survivors saved for the move,
Those unable to keep up
Boxed for the used-book shop.

Folders of forgotten ideas,
Quotes, notes, paraphrases,
Insights, issues, questions,
Opinions and theories,
Spoken to rows and rows
Of so many forgotten faces
After all these years.

Seeming verities,
Now frayed and fading
In the present glare,
Files quietly dustbinned now
After all these years.

Memorabilia off the office noticeboard,
Bare shelves and walls now,

The finality
Of an empty desk,
The door closed
On an empty room.

Dying

Dying is so easy,
There's *absolutely* nothing to it.
All you have to do
Is stay as quiet as eyelids,
As still as waxed fruit in a bowl.

All you have to be
Is a dried leaf on a pillow,
A wrinkled prune in a box.

All the work is done for you.
It's as simple as night-time.

Now living… that's hard!

Hidden Levels

Borre Fen Beauty

Below the curved song
Of the wild wind's rattle,
The rain, in its untiring curiosity,
Runs down heather roots
Deep into a covetous bog,
And finds an arm, encircles a leg,
Explores a torso and flows through
The well-preserved strands of hair
Of a woman drifting in soil
And defying decay
For so many seasons.

The rain seeps through the warp and weft
Of the rough woollen skirt
She wove herself,
Never thinking it would be her shroud,
Then over one uncovered buttock,
And trickles its advance
Through wrinkled valleys of crevassed skin,
Continuing its moist inquisitiveness
Into the marrow of the earth.

Would her husband be pleased
By this bizarre retribution
For his adulterous wife,
Cast out from her kin
And cudgelled into insensibility?

Would he smile in self-righteous satisfaction
To see her being made such an example of
There in front of all those pebbles and worms
For so very long?

And would his rage renew
At the sight of a modern seducer
Caressing her with his eyes,
Invading her most private recesses
With his computer,
And embracing her entirely
With his flash bulb light,
As she lies beneath him,
So motionless and unresponsive?

Mycenean Memory

The path beneath the Lion's Gate
Received our step
As it had Agamemnon's
In the arc of time
That circled his eventful voyage
To a fatal end.

On our walk to the Treasury of Atrius,
A snake, avoiding us,
Slips between hot stones
And is quickly swallowed
By their cool shadows.

On approaching the tomb's mouth
In the head of a hill,
It begins to speak in sounds
Of such disturbing darkness,
Only a spark, lit by the tongues of priests,
Could glow in its core.

Pretending reason,
We allow ourselves to be inhaled
Into its neatly-corbelled cavity,
Where terrifying voices
Are echoing their own repetitions.

In the encircling dimness,
Two Bavarian tourists in *lederhosen*
Sit near the entrance
Cheerfully discussing the events
Of this their first Greek holiday.

Padaung Women

Padaung women
Have very long necks,
No, not from birth,
But stretched by the assaying
Added brass rings
Until, from their shoulders to their heads,
They reclaim the look
Of ancestral dragons,
Whose scaly feet
Raised mythical dust in ancient times.

Padaung women
Freely abandon their first anatomy
To cool the lusts
Of marauding enemies
Who would hardly wish
To carry off a dragon to their homes
On the other side of the horizon.

Daughters continue their mothers' practice
Of elongating their necks,
Believing the tiered sparkle,
As it spoke the sun's language,
Could cause confusion in a tiger's mind,
Thwarting even its most devourish desires.

If a Padaung woman
Breaks the circle
Of her marriage vows,
Her rings are removed,
Causing her extended neck,
Much too long to support her head,
To collapse in a very undragon-like way,
Hardly appealing to any marauding enemy,
And much too lifeless for the appetite
Of even the hungriest of tigers.

Three Women, Abandoned as Children on the Banks of the Amazon, Discover the Men Who Find Them

A long seed-pod,
Pushed by a buzzing sound,
Carries the pale ones,
Like us, but not,
Closer.

They step on the shore
And have no feet!
Nearer they come
They say sounds unlike ours.
We try to keep them in our mouths,
But they fall from us,
And we cannot find them again.

We talk to each other
About their sky-eyes,
Dried-grass hair
And sunlight skins.

They have brought a sharp flat stone
That catches the sun in daylight.
If you pull it across a leaf,
It can quickly make it two.

They have twigs
That suddenly laugh with orange tongues,
And breathe a grey breath
That eats branches black
Until they're completely gone.

Leaves from no trees
Cover them completely
And do not fall from their legs and shoulders.

They give us a big leaf
That almost never ends, and makes us warm.
We throw it to the ground and cry with happiness.

The water's moving
Never carried such floatings before.
Where did they come from?

Suddenly,
A fly, bigger than any bird,
Falls from the sky
And sits on the waters!
Its sound is terrible, terrible!
We try to brush it away from our eyes,
But no... no!
It won't go away!

Resonance

One eye,
Part of a nose,
Half a sensuous mouth
Struggle their perfection
Past jagged omissions
Defacing the sculpted features
Of an Ancient Egyptian princess.

Was her image disfigured
By a spurned lover's wrath,
Or just damaged by fallen columns
In her forgotten tomb?

Is that matchless symmetry
Only the carver's art,
Or the stone echo of a face
So beautiful that,
Despite such harsh interference,
It can still flicker
So perfect a resonance
From such an ancient time?

Mnemonists

Two old men swaying in Finland,
Knee to knee, hand in hand,
Waking wrinkled acts and deeds,
Fingering their treasure
With their tongues.

An Aran Islander,
Rowing his friend's hand,
As they voyage through
A song of lost souls
Doomed by a boat unable to find
The clutch of shore.

Ancient Greek remembrances
Reciting archives
Before written records replaced their services.

The African historian,
Intoning tribal memories,
As drums pace his procession
Of hunts and fallen chieftains,
And the white men who took so many away.

A bard unrolling a tapestry of sagas
For a chieftain and his guests;
Each character in his verse
Blinking in the light
Before being shadowed away, perhaps forever.

The young rote-rhymer,
Hands behind his back,
Speaking more rhythm than sense,
Smiles in ending,
All for the flutter of clapping hands.

The Russian,
Whose eyes capture whatever he sees,
Must write names on bits of paper
And burn them if he wants to forget.

The many things memory nets
Sparkle in the moment's light
Then swim back to the darkness
Where once they were,
And patiently wait to be recalled.

Smiling Soldier

To the infinitely-powerful,
Unlettered and incurably-superstitious
Emperor Qin Shihaung,
Death was always the worm in his thoughts.

He ordered his wisest doctors
To brew a potion
That would make him immortal,
But still he aged,
And the doctors were beheaded.

He dispatched his most-trusted ministers
To the far edges of his empire
To find the secret of eternal life,
But they returned empty-handed
And were also beheaded.

The Emperor then devised a stratagem.
He commanded a clay army of archers,
Horsemen, foot-soldiers and charioteers
To stand forever outside where he lay in his tomb,
And guard him constantly
Against that terrifying force
He believed would rob him
Of what immortality he'd left
While ruling his dark kingdom.

Covered with soil,
The earthenware army
Remained vigilant and loyal
Facing each dark century,

Until a humble farmer's plough
Furrowed their whereabouts,
And archaeologists discovered
Among Emperor Shihaung's thousands
Of standing battalions
One fallen soldier,
Smiling and serene,
As if pleased finally
To be relieved from his post
So he could return
To his wife and children.

Wonders

Winter's Epitaph

The wind adjusts
Diagonals of rain.

Fickle gasps from greenish trees
Echo in April's lost edge.

Stalks signal
The tentative promptness
Of daffodils.

Awakened shadows
Search for their source.

The remorseless soil
Atones only
With its acclaim of tulips.

Cloudward weeds reach into
The earth's bubbling auguries,

As seeds turn to stem
In winter's begrudging epitaph.

Botanists Discover Trees Talk to Each Other

Botanists discover
Trees talk to each other;
No, not exactly in the indicative mood,
But more in an arboreal imperative
Whose scented syntax
Warns others of the caterpillar's will
To devour their very core.

Once the larvae start their attack,
Trees, inferring danger
From the dittos of the worms' assault,
Start their pungent song
Assigning arias of alarm to the winds.

Resplendent neighbours
Soon hear their smell
And respond with their own speechless cry
By defending themselves
With the semantics of their scent.

The rhetoric of the tree's shrill aroma
Is too much for the caterpillars,
Who are forced to leave
In search of less-vocal nourishment.

The trees, now reprieved from the passing menace,
Rest their aromatic voices,
Safe in their silence once more.

Love Story

In the warm coastal waters
That moisten the Equator,
A seahorse drifts deep within
Algal curtains of seagrass,
And waits with expectant eyes.

At last she appears,
Drifting down towards him
On the first shafts of morning light.
Approaching,
She chameleons her colour to his.
They clasp tails, and then,
Disappear across the threshold
Of their watery nuptial bed.

Free of their singularity,
They unite in the arousal of their purpose,
She, in her embrace,
Dispatches embryonic specks of life
Into the harmony of his womb.
He, at the climax of his aria,
Engulfs her notes
In a crescendo of his own.

The seeds of her song
Sound so deep within him,
He must gasp for more breath to sustain them.

She, her finale completed,
Leaves him reluctantly,
To swim back to where she first emerged.
He, no longer alone,
Waits for the growth of their mingling
To flower into a thousand echoes of his form.

Time seeps into the tides
Of the small lives
Stirring in his distended belly
And weighing him down,
As he glides slowly
Through the flow of each day.

Finally, the young fulfil their form
Squirming and twisting into life,
Each nourished by him into growth.

Their self-propelling thrusts
Leave him empty amid voids of fish,
Flashing through the slanted light
That brightens his solitary silence.

Occasionally, females who would, no doubt,
Be receptive to his advances
Drift by his disinterested gaze,
While he floats
Deep within the surrounding sea.

At last she appears,
Drifting down towards him
On the first shafts of morning light.
Approaching,
She chameleons her colour to his.
They clasp tails, and then,
Disappear across the threshold
Of their watery nuptial bed.

Mozart's Starling

Mozart once bought a starling
To help him melody K453.

The bird echoed
Closing doors,
The chiming of the clock,
The crisp clinking of dishes
And cadences of Wolfgang's voice
As he talked to his wife and friends.

Not possessing his master's perfect pitch,
The starling sang in his own birdish tonality,
Unfit for comparison with the sweet sounds
That came so effortlessly from his captor's fingers.

Although Mozart found a melody
Somewhere in the starling's chirping chaos,
Perhaps the bird also taught him
How nature is so very much
What art is not.

Blackbird

A blackbird suffered in my garden this morning.

Ripples of alarm swelled from the dark centre
Of its yellow eye.
Its useless wing a broken catapult
Tucked into its side;
The oracle of its breath
Already foretelling decay.

As I came near,
It hopped away
Searching the fringes of its despair,
Playing a sudden role
In an ancient allegory.

I Was Misled by Rainbows

I always thought rainbows were mawkish things,
Fit only for greeting cards
And misleading children with worthless talk
Of pots of gold guarded by little people;
But then I learned how they really were
Great circles of light
Half-lost below the horizon
And not arcs at all.

I was deceived to believe
Rainbows were thoroughfares
For Iris to walk on,
Delivering messages for the gods,
But then I discovered the sun's light
Was split into colours
Whose hues and order were not negotiable.

I imagined rainbows might be striped serpents
Hunting for the sun's source,
Slipping between rocky clouds
To disappear into a grassy sky,
But then I saw how each snake is never alone,
But watched over by a larger one, just behind.

I was misled by rainbows,
Thinking they were the squall's way
To astonish the dull clouds
With what their greyness could never be;

But then I learned
Only the sun can arc a rainbow,
Conjure its colours,
And make them fall
Where it wills.

A Soft Syncopation

A soft syncopation
Against the inside of my window,
Tells of a brocaded symmetry
And filament feelers
Beating against a sky
Mysteriously made hard.

I cup my hand over
The small heartbeat-flutter,
Holding for a moment
This strayed fragment
From some bigger plan,
Extend my fist
Out the opened window,
Unfold my fingers,
And away it flies.

Woolly Mammoth

The woolly mammoth,
Whose hot breath once smoked Arctic air;
And long curved tusks
Swept prehistoric snows aside
In search of sedges, mosses, grasses,
And shoots of willow, alder and birch,
Was erased long ago.

It only lives now in lines
Etched deep in the sleep of hunters,
Whose stained spears have long been still,
Or scratched on the walls
Of Lascaux and Rouffignac.

Vagaries of seasons,
Too many hunting parties or both
May have caused its loss.

We know only that,
Like the sabre-toothed tiger and giant deer,
This lumbering creature
Was only a brief visitor to sentience.

My Cat is Confounded

My cat is confounded
By the silver-streaked mystery
That falls from the bathtub tap
And disappears into a dark circle.

It beckons the transparent form
To act as solid as other things it knows,
But is only answered by a damp stain
On its soft grey paw.

A Slick Con Man

A slick con man,
With a black shirt and star-speckled tie,
Seamlessly persuaded me,
With his innocent crescent smile,
That he alone could heal the hurt
Of the long day's abrasions.

Foolishly,
I was completely taken in,
And before I knew it,
He'd robbed me of everything I owned.

I awoke to find he'd quickly left town
Without even leaving a forwarding address.

But the very next night
He reappeared
With those soft deceptions
And that ingratiating smile
I'd known for so long.

Unable to learn from my mistakes,
So soon and once again,
I let him lead me to that dark place
I could never know,
But would one day
Always be my home.

Protests

Marx Under the Nile

A small reed-boat
Bravely parts the dark waters of the underworld,
As the last cries of mourners are lost in the cleft wake
Trailing from an oar intruding
In that flow beneath time itself,
And as far as the distant land
Of the great god Osiris.

The boat's privileged passenger
Smiles beneath his bandages,
Secure in knowing all his earthly luxuries
Will continue to be his
Throughout the sunless days to come,
As they always have,
With the certainty of ripples
Ordained each evening to reach the shore
With their golden cargo from each dying sun.

The lookout in the bow,
Put to death with the rest of the crew
To accompany his master on this voyage
Unsweetened by thoughts of return,
Looks into the darkness for the first sign
Of the edge of the end of all things,
Listening for the landfall sound
Of the far bank's welcome.

Two of the crew subdue the flapping sail's response
To a persistent wind,
While in the stern,
A grim-faced oarsman steers his steady course
But asks himself:

'Why am I plucked too soon
from all in the world
that was sweet to me?

'If I am now no more
than a cipher's centre,
why must I slave for so little gain?

'Is this all I was fashioned for,
to be embalmed in the same tasks
without end, to watch my master
indulge himself forever?'

Slowly, he opens his hand
And lets the steering oar slip from his fingers
And sink soundlessly into the darkest of all waters.

Gradually, the small reed-boat drifts off its course
And out into the common, uncharted sea
Of classless oblivion.

Columbus's Wake

Take back your Bible and give it back to our oppressors.
They need its moral precepts more than we because, since
Christopher Columbus, South America has had imposed on
it, by force, a culture, a language, a religion and values which
belong to Europe.

A letter from the Aymara Indians of Peru to Pope John
Paul II before his visit there in 1985.

Slowly as centuries,
Like trampled weeds
Twisting toward light,
They increase from under the heel
Of those first pale oppressors
Whose shining armour covered dark lusts,
Whose tongues spoke in iron,
Trumpeting His name while defiling it,
Searching for a golden Eden
And finding only a sweltering jungle
For planting emblazoned banners,
Snapping crisply against cloudless skies,
Louder than the cries of those
Forced to swallow the soil of their fathers.

In the half-millennium
Since the glisten of a white god
Was seen to be only the patina of corruption,
New *conquistadores* still celebrate old atrocities
And send their shaman and his book of spells
To remind the remnants of a people
That the dull shine of their native gold
Is still the counterfeit of another's currency,

That they can still be scythed down
In the squalor of their cities,
Their idols still taken from them
And melted down to bulge the stomachs of the overfed.

And still they're made to stare
Bewildered, poor and helpless,
Far out to the horizon
At Columbus's wake.

Timor Equation

Some epauletted Brother gave his breath away.

Emily Dickinson

Young men and women,
On a small screen I watch,
Serge in righteous anger
Down the main street of a small island
Off the coast of Australia,
Banners and chants their garments of protest,
Worn proudly in the sunlight.

They stride to the cemetery
Where brothers, sisters and friends,
Picked up from where they fell,
Have all been eased into the ground,
And now are only names on cold slabs,
And pale pictures in the minds of those
Left to speak again
Those words that crossed the speech of the fallen;
Oppression, Liberation, Freedom.

Suddenly, uniformed men appear,
Faceless as always in firing squads.
The rasp of shots,
People fall, others run in all directions.

A young man is hit.
He makes his way to the cemetery,
And falls to the ground.
A companion cushions his friend's head.

In the confusion and carnage,
A television cameraman stops,
Zooms in on the young man
With an obscene sunset
Slowly spreading across his white shirt
As he gasps in the graveyard,

Almost ready now
To join that long procession
Of all those before him
Who gave their breath away to prove
That inequitable equation
In which a small cipher of lead
In the hands of oppressors
Easily outweighs
All the abundance of heart
And magnitude of mind
Of those oppressed.

Sarajevo Zoo

The keepers have fled
From Sarajevo Zoo.

Chimps, morose from hunger,
Listen only to the chatter
Of automatic-weapon fire.

Elephants lift their heavy heads
At each blast of shells
Gnawing at buildings nearby.

Giraffes, propped up by cool concrete walls,
Sink quietly to the floor.

Hippos nudge the soil of their dusty pond,
Searching for something green.

Birds that can no longer fly,
Are too weak to preen their infested plumage,
As lice take command.

Each passing day, no keeper comes with food,
Or cleans out the cages.

Small protruding eyes stare out through bars,
As the lion eats his mate.

The Crime of Capital Punishment

The self-righteous wrench of a noose,
Jolt of current, toxic air or poisoned injection
In the name of an ancient vengeance,
Does not outweigh
The outcome of passion's uncharted logic
Or even the most warped syllogisms of evil.

How can such punishment
Commit the same crime it condemns;
Taking the breath of one
Too deep in derangement
To grasp the simple truth
Of how wrong it is
To contradict life?

Uffizi Alteration

Asleep in scholars' minds for so long,
And hidden behind a veil
Of disinterest by the public,
della Notti's *Birth of Christ*
And Manfredi's *La Buona Ventura*
Were suddenly brushed away by a b*ravura* stroke,
(Whose dark technique
These artists would have quickly recognised)
And exploded out of sight forever.

A mother, father, their two children
As well as someone else passing by.
Were, themselves, erased so well
Not even their names appeared
In the evening papers.

Last Stand Tableau

A soldier's gaping mouth,
On a face of no nobility,
Is turned toward the hot Nebraska sky,
Arrows planted red
In the fear-soaked gullies
Of his blue, 7th Cavalry shirt.

Fallen across him,
A Cheyenne brave,
With a small circular emblem oozing red
Across his buckskin.
His upturned white eyes
Have lost the grassy plains
Where ancestors, for so many seasons,
Speared the buffalo's thunder.

Above them, a soldier, pistol blazing,
Eyes shaped by terror,
Sees his last sight;
A palomino, its rider's war-bonnet
Fluttering against an uneventful sky,
And then the swift arc of a tomahawk.

Whoops and cries, screams of pain,
The bark of rifles and whoosh of arrows,
All scented with smells of gunpowder
And fresh blood,

A dazed and seated bugler
Sounds a demented charge for unhorsed men,
As they fire at flocks of Sioux
Circling the hill above Little Big Horn,
Swooping down for the kill,

A standard stuck in the ground nearby
Bears the bitter fruit
Of red, white and blue tatters,

Calm chevalier in the centre of the carnage,
General George Armstrong Custer,
Fresh from his Gettysburg triumphs,
Has deserted his fellow officers
To snatch at a glory they all might have shared.

His bold plan to capture women and children
From their wigwams, to be ransomed
By their men's return to the Reservation,
Has gone terribly wrong.

Surprised instead
By a force of fighting braves,
Custer now stands on his last hill,
Head uncovered,
Yellow hair streaming out behind him,
Pistol in hand,
Straining to sight his next target
In the smoky mayhem,
Surrounded by an ornate golden frame
From which he can never escape.

He had even hoped to be President,
But never thought
He'd have to share his fame forever
With such absurdly aboriginal names
As Sitting Bull and
Crazy Horse of the Oglalas.

I am Unimpressed by the Universe

I am unimpressed by the universe.

All that endless nothing,
Those black holes and countless stars
May tug some people off their couches,
But for me,
Nothing is as awe-inspiring
As greed!

Now there's a power
That can tip the world itself,
Turn hearts into anti-matter,
Devour whole lives, species, forests and populations
Like a flame, leaving only ashes in gratitude.

It fouls entire oceans, changes climates,
Sucks away the very air we breathe;
And, contradicting all the laws of physics,
Always takes much more that it can ever use.

More terrifyingly vast, remote,
Cold, bleak, lifeless, distant and lonely
Than any mere universe wallpapered with stars
And tastelessly decorated
With the moon's fingernail sweetness;
Greed is lit by its own stormy sun,
Its ceaseless energy always in perpetual motion.

As for the universe,
I'm unimpressed, most of all,
By the way something so very big
Can only manage to answer our desperate questions
With the dumb silence
Of its distant galaxies.

Others

Could I?

For Beva

Could skin forget its hold,
Or veins leave their bones to become spiders' webs?

Could the rhetoric of insects drown out
The cloud-filled thunder, or rain rise to the sky?

Could trees leave their roots
And dance to the music of their leaves,
Or cells be inept and forget their purpose?

Could sunsets stop to criticise
The hues of their luminous syntax,
Or flowers question their petals' pattern?

Could streams flow backwards
And be strangers to mountains,
Or birds turn into snowflakes and melt in mid-air?

Could numbers forget calculation,
Or symmetry defy its twin?

Could I ever leave you?

Wittgenstein's Fly

The buzz of my wings
Burnishes this barrier
Into a sheen
That stops the glassy sky
From its blueness.

All the facets of my eyes
Useless in seeing
What keeps me from what
I clearly see.

Walking upside down
Of no help to freedom
From my cylindrical prison.

My taut reflexes unstrung.
There are no threats in solitude.

Each entrance must be an exit.
Each solution finds a question.
Each effect trails to its cause.
But how to escape?

Outside the bottle,
Watching my vexed and futile efforts,
How easy to talk of *truth*.

Logician's Reprieve

A crocodile snatched a baby
From a river-bank.
When its mother implored
For her child's return,
A logician's reprieve
Was all she received.

The crocodile, well past its mealtime,
Stated that if the mother could truly say
What he, with her child neatly sandwiched in his jaws,
Was about to do,
She would win the bargain, and the baby back too.

The mother exclaimed, in a panic
That he would soon sing a toothful lullaby
Using her baby as the melody!

The crocodile,
Thinking the baby as good as digested,
Guffawed that a released baby would only prove
How very false the mother's Wordsworth,
And that she Auden't to have said what wasn't true
Because now he'd won the bargain and the baby too.

No, the mother stymied,
He could not just Nash his grimace,
For an eaten child would only prove
What she'd said entirely true,
And it was she who'd won the bargain
And the baby back too.

The crocodile wondered what Shelley do,
But we'll never know if the scales of his honour
Weighed sufficiently heavy or light
To unbalance his ordinarily-quite-enormous appetite.

Crossed Words

I like the way crossword puzzles
Make me remember
Words I forgot I knew,
The ones put away
Long ago in boxes somewhere
So covered with dust
You could write your name on them.

I especially like the way that
Rustic glimmer,
Demoted grottoes,
Unicorn brigades,
Tee-pee Venus,
Safari charades,

And other words
That never met before,
Suddenly discover,
They have, at least,
One thing in common.

Searching for an Author

He is an impetuous,
Half-moustached man
Always in the midst of things,
Always interrupting
Whatever others have to say.

She is all curve and mystery,
Standing at the edge of a crowd,
Perpetually puzzled and always escorted
By a small speck of a man.

Two pompous gentlemen
Position themselves
Just before some speech is about to begin,
And even though they've heard it all before,
They insist attentively on respectful silence.

Him!
You can quickly see how thin
And excitable he is.
Sometimes he even astonishes himself,
Realising he may be over-reacting to things
Much of the time.

These two are good listeners.
No matter what gossip or
Private information they hear,
They know how to keep a secret
Entirely between themselves.

The small dark man knows them all,
And each one has the greatest respect for him.
You can easily see that's true
By the way just the sight of him
Can put a full stop
To all of their surge and rumble.

Language Learners

The limits of my language is the limit of my world.

Shaping sounds,
Sounding shapes,
The language learners,
Like misinformed archaeologists,
Are busy fitting the wrong shards
Onto the right pots,
Searching for forms whose variations hint
At some unknown perfection.

Shaping sounds,
Sounding shapes,
They the seekers,
We the moulders of an ancient ware
Whose glazed lustre holds
The colour and sparkle of our brightest voices.

Shaping sounds,
Sounding shapes,
These gentle intruders sift through our soil,
Discovering delight
As each fragment finds its place
In those patterns
That limit our world.

Shaping sounds,
Sounding shapes,
The language learners dig through strata,
Recording their inventory,
Delving downward

Through the alluvial wrinkles of pronouns,
The geological shifting of the past continuous,
The bedrock of the present simple,
The fissures of the future,
And the moist subsidence of the conditional.

Shaping sounds,
Sounding shapes,
They return to the surface
With a cargo of discovery
To swell their collection,
Until tongues, like flicking fingers,
Can make our paradigms of clay
Ring with the sound
Of their moulded wholeness.

Xerxes

Sing loudly in lamentation
Notes plaintive and discordant,
Fortune and joy have left me
And sorrow takes their place.

      Aeschylus, *The Persians*

I

Heroes' ashes at Marathon
Had hardly crusted cool
Before the Persian chimera,
Uncoiled once more,
Its sides bristling with spears,
Scales catching pieces of sun,
Its sinews stretching
To the farthest horizon
With trousered Scythians
And their curved daggers and pointed caps;
Ethiopians painted half-chalk, half-vermilion,
Helmeted with horses' skulls;
Indians in cotton tunics,
Carrying long cane bows;
Thracians in multi-coloured cloaks,
Their wooden shields
Covered in magical signs;
Assyrians in belted robes,
With their bronze helmets and battle axes;
All behind the Persian Immortal Ten Thousand,
Immediately able to replace
Any limb hacked-off in battle.

Listen to the trumpets' rasp!
Hear the marching feet,
Slow percussion of drums,
Shuffle of oxen, horses' hooves,
And bangles of women
Alongside the slithering legion.
See the puffs of dust they raise
Clouding their way to the Hellespont.

At the serpent's head is Xerxes.
His clipped black beard,
Royal turban and regal stare
Only a thin mask
Hiding his loss of youthful fire,
His slip from innocence to indolence,
Now leaving an unsteady throne
To quench his dead father's
Thirst for vengeance,
Now setting out
In search of Greek corpses
To pave a path back to his peoples' hearts,
And smooth the wound of Marathon
To an empire that stretched
From the Sphinx to sight of the Ganges.

II

On to the Hellespont,
Galleys lashed side-by-side
To bridge the waters
For the hungry serpent
Bound to gorge on Hellas,
But the night-waves' wild mischief
Tears the bridge apart.
Xerxes enraged,
Orders three thousand lashes
Across the water's back,
Raising welts of foam,
Its banks branded for complicity.

And the impudent sea manacled into captivity,
As a new bridge spans
The chastened and humbled waters.

III

Macedonia watches
As the chimera's shadow
Cools sun-soaked stones.
Even the Olympians are impressed
To see mortals and beasts
Drink whole rivers dry.

By Thessaly's edge at Thermopylae Pass
Persian spies watch Leoniades' Spartans,
Naked as if preparing for a race,
Grooming their hair and stretching their limbs,
Aware the serpent is near
And about to spring.

On it comes!
Rushing forward,
Snorting fire and terrible sounds;
But the Pass is too narrow,
And the reptile, scraping its sides,
Recoils in pain,
As the first drops of its blood
Fall on foreign soil.
Again it lunges its scaly bulk
And again recoils in pain,
Until a traitor shows the way
Around the gap;
And the beast's fiery breath
Turns Spartans to cinders
Whose glow will never cool,
Despite Xerxes' command
To crush Leoniades' body
Into fragments for the ground.

IV

In Athens,
The Oracle tells of 'salvation behind wooden walls'.
Some stay to shield Athena's temple with sticks;
But soon the chimera is on the Acropolis.
No one is spared its fiery breath.
Its smoke is seen with sadness
By those in the Straits of Salamis,
Waiting patiently for Xerxes' armada
To heedlessly pass Soúnion's warning finger
And slip into Poseidon's realm
Where a snare is set.

V

On a hill high above the sea,
A throne is brought for Xerxes,
Its four legs tipped with lions' heads,
Each gnawing at the ground of a land
Unused to the tyrannies of the East;
An eagle's view fitting for a mighty king
As he looks down on his prey
About to be so easily devoured.

Deceived the Greek's fleet is fleeing,
The chimera, thirsting for carnage,
Takes to the sea
And swims into the narrow straits,
Cupped by close shores.
Only then do the agile sharks attack.

VI

Rammed hulls,
Catapulted burning oil,
Sparks, flames, cries,
Black smoke, crushed wood,
Masts and tangled rigging fall,
Smashed oars, shouts, screams,

Calls of the drowning,
Blood running down broken hulls
Stains the wreckage-strewn sea.

The sleek Greek sharks tear at the flesh
Of a beast too large
For so small a space,
Its claws broken, teeth smashed, tail severed,
Choking for air, the chimera's own thrashing
Sinks its vast bulk
Deep into the Aegean's crimson-stained waves.

VII

Xerxes' arrogant mask has fallen from his face.
The flotsam of corpses
And mangled skeleton of his fleet
Have overcome him with disbelief.
The lions on the legs of his throne
Are left abandoned and hungry
As Xerxes flees from the spectacle,
Seeing the chimera dying in pain
And knowing the smoke from Salamis has eclipsed
The reign of Xerxes' son of Darius.

The young king will return to Persia
And a palace of intrigue.
He will feel the knife from a hidden hand
Cut away his life
And leave him to the debris of history.

As fundamental darkness falls on all his lands,
It is the sunrise and glory of the West!

The Parachutist's Wedding

For Erika and Wilf

My darling girl
And her friend of the clouds
Have met in a new sky
High above their loneliness,
To link hands
In that longest fall,
With us all,
Their feet piercing clouded hope
And troubled crosswinds,
High above an undiscovered landscape
Only years will bring.

Now they float in a new formation
For only two,
Slowly down through days and seasons
Safe in each other's touch.

And we who look up and watch them today,
Wish them courage in the jump,
The clearest of skies,
The best of views,
A way through storms,
Happiness in the fall,
And the softest and safest of landings.

The Rape of the Lock

Browsing through
Poetry books
From a library shelf,
I opened one to a random page.

To my surprise,
A lock of silky blonde hair
Fell out of the book
And onto the floor.

I picked it up
And rolled it slowly
Across my fingers.

How *poetic*, I thought.

The Ol' Model-T Ford and the Steam Train

The nasal whine of a blues harp
Brings me down to the street below
My French Quarter balcony
To see an old black man walking along,
A silver harmonica cupped in his hand,
And breathing sounds from somewhere
Words could never travel.

He finds me watching him and stops to talk;
And soon takes an old piece of soiled paper
Out of his frayed shirt-pocket,
Unhinges it and shows me the white man's contract
For a session played but never paid.

'*That's not right*,' he says,
Looking at me imploringly.

'No it isn't,' I say
Shaking my head
From side to side in agreement.

His eyes study me from a distant country
Where I'm the enemy's envoy,
Here for a moment's truce in this clearing.

'*Do you wanna hear da Model-T Ford
and da Steam Train?*' he asks me,
Smiling with a few teeth missing.

I nod respectfully.

He slowly cranks up the Model-T,
Then it's racing towards the level crossing,
Trying to get there
Before the train gets there first;
But not even the train's shrill whistle
Can stop the car now.

The crash sends his fleshy lips furiously racing
Up and down the harp,
As the sound of crushed metal and shattered glass
Echoes along the New Orleans street.

He takes the harmonica out of his mouth
For the moment,
A look of satisfaction at the smile on my face.

'*See ya 'round sometime*,' he says,
Then puts the harmonica back in his mouth,
And walks away, playing as he goes.

Crossroads

Béla Bartók, the great Hungarian composer, often lamented that the folk tradition of his country was a candle flame carried into a windy night.

On a field trip with his portable recorder, he arrived at an inn in a remote mountain village. There he was told of a woman named Olga whose voice was without equal in the region.

Asking where she could be found, he learned that Olga brought her cows down from the high hills each evening, always at the same time, always arriving at the same crossroads.

Bartók climbed the hills with his recorder and waited at the spot where he and Olga would meet.

Cows soon appeared, followed by an elderly woman, her grey hair tucked under a *babushka*, and a walking stick in her hand.

'Good evening woman,' Bartók said. 'Are you Olga?'

'No,' the woman replied.

'But surely you are Olga, the singer the villagers praise so highly?'

'No,' the woman answered with a warm smile and bid the composer a good evening as she walked down the dirt road and into the twilight.

Bartók, confused and disappointed, stood alone in the mild breeze and fading light, watching the woman as she slowly disappeared. When she was almost completely out of sight, she began singing... magnificently!

P.V.S.[2]

Becalmed by a lost breeze,
Adrift on drops from a tube,
For twenty years,
Only wisps of breath
And the rise and fall of her chest
To distinguish her from dead,

No faces familiar,
No scent of bedside flowers,
No voices to hear or footsteps to recognise,

Arms contracted, legs extended, jaws clenched,
Teeth capped with rubber covers
To keep her from biting her tongue,

Visitors few then fewer,
One-way conversations soon overcome by silence,
Still the monthly cheques arrive
For the drip, drip, drip,
And the rise and fall of her chest.

Clouds elaborate their patterns each day
Across an unseen sky while her hair is combed,
Soiled bedclothes removed, body washed,
And the drip, drip, drip,
And the rise and fall of her chest,

---

[2] Permanent Vegetable State.

Word was,
She was a lively young woman
Who hated hospitals,
The sort who'd have turned off her switch
In an instant, had she only known
Of her numb voyage
Without hope of ever reaching a shore.

Judges ruled, family finally agreed,
The nursing home spokesperson objected,
Lawyers debated, priests argued,
Pro-life supporters protested,

Now, after all this time,
A gentle wind will carry her away
Once they've turned off the darkness,
To finally reach another shore.

Hawaiian Cane Toad

The sugar cane grub was a devastator in Australia. Sugar cane farmers were beside themselves watching it devour their crops right there in front of them. But news came from Hawaii of a grub-eating toad who could be imported to answer all their prayers.

Soon a large box arrived from aloha land with a delegation attached to it. Inside were toads who had been persuaded they were taking a trip to a grub-filled paradise across the Pacific, where they could have unending helpings of their favourite delicacy until they exploded.

Once in Queensland, the toads jump out of their boxes. One look at their large warty heads, bulging eyes and slimy, bumpy green bodies would be enough to send even the most repugnant of reptiles slithering to the mirror to admire itself.

Hopping towards the sugar cane, the toads eat everything in sight; and just as they reach the faltering stalks, they fall into a deep, satiated sleep. Meanwhile, the grubs, just waking and ravenous, climb over the sleeping toads, eat their fill then return to their sugary dreams.

In the morning, the toads, disinterested in inactive grubs, continue their gastronomic rampage. Little that is green or moves escapes their long venomous tongues. And if something larger happens to swallow them, it's quickly poisoned by the toads, who are vindictive even in digestion.

Kookaburras mysteriously fall senseless to the ground. Dogs and cats moan and are no more; and kangaroos, like overturned tables, lie dead on their backs all across the landscape.

Those who have witnessed the Hawaiian cane toads at sex say the way they go about it would make even the most devout believer seriously wonder what God could have been thinking of. Although no stunned voyeur has yet been persuaded to describe exactly what they've seen, one observer was heard to comment,

'Well, what's lost in elegance is sure made up for by the female, who can lay forty thousand eggs at a time!'

By now, the toads feel so much at home that they begin inviting themselves into people's houses. Jumping on plates, past jabs of knives and forks, they devour whatever is for dinner; and if a household pet comes to the rescue, the toad's spiteful venom soon leaves it stiff and cold on the checkerboard lino on the kitchen floor.

People whose cars happen to coincide with a toad crossing the road seldom hear the squish, but soon smell an odour so severe, the scent of all the sewers of Queensland could easily be mistaken for eau de cologne.

By this time, the almost-loveable sugar grub has been discouraged from its diet of cane by a newly-invented spray, souring the taste of its favourite dish.

Meanwhile, the Hawaiian cane toad is multiplying at an alarming rate. A delegation from Queensland is busy building boxes.

Thrift Shop Window

Has-beens,
Recently returned by popular demand,
Perform daily in the thrift shop window.

Tanned and wrinkled high-heeled shoes,
With sullen straps,
Step it out behind handbags on the brink of mildew.
Knitted baby booties and matching bonnet
Do their *Do-you-remember-when?* routine in the corner,
Just in front of the limp wedding gown
Divorced from its box in the attic.

Also on the bill,
A box of seashell-shaped soap
That never knew the sound of the sea;
An exhausted electric bar-heater
Trailing its frayed lead behind it;
LPs of singers no one would remember
Well enough to forget;
Mills and Boon paperbacks with such titles as
Maggie's Last Temptation,
A Summer's Passion and
Yesterday's Only Tomorrow;
A plaque with Souvenir de Lourdes
Written under a small,
Pale-blue plaster statue
Of a perpetually-praying Virgin;
And an English country scene
Peeling off a puzzle box,
With only one or two pieces missing.

Reluctant to be old,
Barely able to perform,
Has-beens at show time,
Brought back by popular demand
From recently-cancelled engagements.

G.P.S.

For Sandy Earle

Sailors adrift on cascading surf,
Motorists still in clotted traffic,
Walkers pathless in unknown places,
Need no longer be misplaced or missing,
Unseen or unknown.

All invisibly tied
To techno-dots in the sky,

Eluding panic,
Estranged from confusion,
Emptied of helplessness,

Their *global positioning system*'s little screen
Shows them
Exactly where they are.

And like some fading species,
The quiet terror of being lost
Will soon be
No more than
A barely-remembered curiosity.

Burden and Advice

I

The great jazz drummer Buddy Rich
Lay on his deathbed.
A priest attending him
Asked if there was anything
That burdened his mind
And troubled his final moments.

'*Yes*,' Buddy replied faintly.
'*Country and Western music*,'

II

When Dizzy Gillespie,
Who'd made it through the melody,
Flown with the Bird,
And was well on his way into the coda,
Was asked by a young trumpeter
For advice on the best way
To play the instrument,
Dizzy replied,

'*Son, first you hold your trumpet*
right out there in front of you,
take a long look at it, and say,
"Trumpet, I'm yours"!'

Printed in the United Kingdom
by Lightning Source UK Ltd.
901